Reprints of Economic Classics

THOMAS SPENCE
AND HIS CONNECTIONS

THOMAS SPENCE

(Photographic enlargement of one of his tokens now in the British Museum Coin and
Medal Department)

THOMAS SPENCE

AND HIS CONNECTIONS

BY

OLIVE D. RUDKIN

REPRINTS OF ECONOMIC CLASSICS

AUGUSTUS M. KELLEY · PUBLISHERS
NEW YORK · 1966

First Published 1927

Library of Congress Catalogue Card Number

65 - 26378

Printed in the United States of America
by Sentry Press, New York, N. Y. 10019

PREFACE

WHEN Miss Olive D. Rudkin was preparing a thesis on Thomas Spence for the degree of M.A. in the University of London, I had the pleasure of acting as her director of studies. The examiners, eventually, found that Miss Rudkin had thrown some new light on Spence's career, had made use of documents never before used, and had contributed a valuable bibliography. But her present essay is a vast improvement on the relative crudity and incompleteness of its first form. It is, I think, by far the most adequate account of Spence and his doings, his ideas, and his spiritual relations, that has yet appeared. Spence is an interesting person, and even an amusing one. He is interesting as an early advocate of socialistic experiments with the land, as a forerunner, in some respects, of Owenism and of later land nationalizers. He is interesting, too, as an example of how ignorance fosters and neglect and opposition exasperate fanaticism. Ignorant he was and fanatical, largely by reason of his ignorance, confused by many emotions, and ridiculously sure that he was right. But if a life of desperate poverty utterly devoted to the service of humanity be a saintly life, then Thomas Spence was a saint. His passionate desire for justice, his passionate sympathy with the oppressed and disinherited, his engaging faith that he had found the sure and only remedy for all ills, distinguished and isolated him in an indifferent and contemptuous world. Yet the seed he scattered did not, as Miss Rudkin shows, fall only on stony ground. It may be said of him, as of all of us, that his activities had not the results he hoped for, but results they certainly had.

In dealing with this great little man, Miss Rudkin is mistress of her subject and never superior to it. She has never been even tempted to commit either the unpardonable sin of patronizing, or the unpardonable sin of sneering. She is watchful and balanced, a little in love with her hero and always sympathetic. Quietly and irresistibly, in this study of a very interesting and a very lovable man, Miss Rudkin communicates to the reader her own sympathy and understanding.

J. W. ALLEN.

AUTHOR'S FOREWORD

THIS biography of Thomas Spence has been compiled mainly from his tracts, from the biographies of his friends : T. Evans, " Life of Mr. Thomas Spence," 1821 ; Eneas Mackenzie, " Memoir of T. Spence," 1826 ; " A Descriptive and Historical Account . . . of Newcastle-upon-Tyne," 1827 ; Thomas Bewick, " A Memoir of Thomas Bewick," 1862 ; Allen Davenport, " Life Writings and Principles of Thomas Spence," 1836 ; and from the MSS. of Francis Place (British Museum Add. MSS. 27808 and 27809, and the Place Journals).

Francis Place had intended to write a biography of Spence, and about 1830–31 he was busy collecting material, but even then he failed to get into touch with Spence's relatives either in Newcastle or London. He failed, for instance, to find any trace of Spence's second wife.

The information from these sources has been supplemented by reference to the " Annual Register," Hansard, the Home Office papers, the Newcastle and London newspapers and magazines of the period, Bamford's " Life of a Radical," and the publications of William Hone. For the comparison between the thought of Spence and Owen I have depended upon Robert Owen, " Life of R. Owen " (1857–58), and his tracts generally, especially those published

1812–21. But I owe a great deal to Frank Podmore's "Life of R. Owen," 1906.

A personal visit to Newcastle was made more fruitful through Professor Hearnshaw's "Short History of Newcastle," and Reid's "Handbook."

Professor Foxwell's bibliography of socialistic writings and his Introduction to the translation of Anton Menger's "Right to the Whole Produce of Labour" (1897), were of great assistance to me. Mr. A. W. Waters, "Trial of Thomas Spence" (1917, privately printed), has also proved most helpful and suggestive.

I should like specially to thank Professor Graham Wallas, not only for the use that I have been able to make of his "Life of Place," but for the help that he has so kindly given to me whenever I have asked him for advice; and Professor J. W. Allen, who suggested this line of research to me, and who, besides reading my MS., has both helped and directed my studies.

O. D. RUDKIN.

CONTENTS

THOMAS SPENCE

CHAPTER I

EARLY DAYS

THOMAS SPENCE was born at Newcastle-on-Tyne in
1750. He was thirteen years old when the Peace of
Paris was signed and Britain became mistress of her
first Empire. He was in the vigour of young manhood when the quarrel with America opened up
fundamental political questions.

Newcastle is a town with a personality, a personality
that is surely bred from its military and commercial
importance. It is not as easy to perceive personality
in some towns as it is in Newcastle. Perhaps the
fact that Newcastle is not unending helps perception—
there are moors within view. Or the Tyne, the con-
troller and director of the city's life, may help. Then
Newcastle has not lost as many links with the past
as some big commercial cities. The Quay, the Chares,
the city churches, though much altered, belong to old
as well as modern times. Some old houses stand in
the Sandhill opposite the Guildhall. The Keep of the
New Castle is still the guardian of the city's commerce.
From the Guildhall one looks to a small blue pane
in the window of an old house and reads romance.

From the top of the Keep one gazes down on main-line trains rushing through the Castle courtyard.

When Spence was born, Newcastle, for all its importance, was little more in appearance than a country town. Its population numbered less than 30,000.[1] The Sandhill, once a recreation ground, was the centre of the town's activities. It was the Market Square, and on market-days the sellers set up their booths, or stalls, in front of the gabled houses where important citizens dwelt. The mayor, the corporation, and the various guild officials controlled the destinies of the town from the Guildhall. At the foot of the Side, a steep, dingy lane leading from the market-place, the butchers, cheesemongers, and bacon-dealers haggled with their customers. Half-way up, the Dog Leap Stairs led, as now, to the Castle. Then, the Castle was surrounded with a huddle of miserable houses and filthy lanes. At the head of the Side there was a refuse dump. Wealthy merchants lived and sold their wares in Pilgrim Street. Close by the Gothic Church of All Saints looked down upon the river and the Quay.

The Quay, the centre of the shipping life of the town, was narrow, dirty, and inconvenient. Some of the eighteenth-century houses still border the Quay. In Spence's time they must have been uncomfortably near the water's edge. Twenty narrow Chares, crowded with the houses of the poor, led from the Quay into the town.

At close quarters, the town would have seemed squalid and dirty to modern eyes, but from a distance

[1] The census returns for 1801 give 28,294.

it must have been a beautiful sight. One would look along the " bonny coaly Tyne," from the old bridge with its houses and shops, to the great curve that the river takes, and after idly watching the river-craft, the keels and the sailing-ships, one would note the red brick houses with their gables and dormer windows, the green of the gardens, the Keep, the tower of St. Nicholas's Church, and, beyond the town wall, the moors. John Wesley said that if he were not " journeying toward Heaven, he could not wish for a more pleasant abiding place than Newcastle." [1]

For signs of progress and prosperity in the town, the visitor would observe the activities connected with the shipyards and the Quay. He would inspect the houses and shops in Pilgrim Street and Westgate Street. The number of booksellers' shops would attract his attention, and he could not fail to notice the newspapers, magazines and educational works for sale there.[2]

The newspapers are photographs illustrating the life of the town. Notices of cock-fights, highway robberies, public whippings, stolen and strayed cattle, runaway slaves and transportations, are mixed up with advertisements of lectures on electricity or of Signor Lunardi's balloon ascent (1786). Each paper has its literary corner in which extracts from current publications are quoted and notices of new books appear. Each newspaper proprietor was a bookseller and

---

[1] Reid's " Handbook," p. 2.
[2] *Newcastle Courant*, published 1711. *Newcastle Journal*, published 1739. Three other newspapers were published between 1750 and 1800. *Newcastle General Magazine*, published 1747. Five other magazines were published 1750–1800.

publisher, and made a speciality of educational books, almanacs and diaries. Each added to his profits by the sale of hair-powder, cosmetics and quack medicines. When some ship's load of tea or coffee was put up for sale, perhaps " by candle," [1] the proprietor would buy up what he could, and presently would advertise tea and coffee amongst his wares.

The town was well provided with schools. Among others, there were the Grammar School, founded in the sixteenth century, and St. Ann's School in 1682. There were, too, some fine hospitals.

In the latter half of the eighteenth century great changes took place in Newcastle. The population was increasing, and with it the number of houses. In 1763 the streets were first lighted—candles were used for the purpose. Some of the slum areas were cleared around St. Nicholas's Church. The pulling down of the wall began, and the Quay was widened and improved. Better coaches were put on the road and a speedier service was maintained. Public baths were opened (in 1781) and the number of hospitals was increased. The Assembly Rooms were built in 1774. As the great flood of 1771 destroyed the fourteenth-century bridge, a new one was constructed. This was completed by 1781. New streets were being cut.

Yet even with these alterations Newcastle did not begin to wear its modern aspect until the nineteenth century.

The Spences were not natives of Newcastle. Spence's

---

[1] An auction at which the lot goes for the highest bid made before the fall of the wick.

father came to Newcastle from Aberdeen about 1739. After following his trade of netmaker for a few years, he opened a booth upon the Sandhill for the sale of hardware goods. He was twice married, and had nineteen children by the two marriages. His second wife was Margaret Flet, a native of the Orkneys. She was an industrious woman, and kept a stall for the sale of stockings. When Thomas, her son, was born, June 21, 1750, the family was living on the Quayside, where the poorer people resided.

All his life Spence was miserably poor. His parents had a hard struggle to maintain themselves and their large family.

"Advancing in years," he found himself and his father's family "in continual difficulties and embarrassments," in spite of all their "economy and industry." [1] He had little education given to him. He relates how his father taught him and his brother to read the Bible, how he made his sons stand by him while he worked, and how he then questioned them on what they had read. Thus his children learnt to reflect.[2]

The rest of his education was left to himself. "Had I been learned," he explains to the Jury in 1801, "I would perhaps have wrote in Latin. But knowing but one language I am obliged, like the prophets and great men of antiquity, to write in my mother tongue." [3]

His lesson-book was the Bible, his chief source of instruction was the Old Testament; Moses and Samson

[1] Spence, "Important Trial," p. 56.
[2] Spence, "Interesting Conversation" in "Rights of Man," 1793. "Important Trial."
[3] Spence, "Important Trial," p. 60.

were his favourite heroes. He rarely mentions the New Testament, though he had studied Revelation, evidently as completing the cycle of prophetic books.

There is little precise information as to the actual books read by Spence. His " Pigs' Meat " (1793 . . .) consists of extracts from books read by Spence during the preceding twenty years. A list of authors and of books can be made from the three volumes. The length or number of the extracts given from the works of any writer is proof in itself of some acquaintance with the works, but one proviso must be made. It is more than likely that the bulk of Spence's book-knowledge came from the newspapers, as a cursory glance at their literary corners suggests. There were in these literary corners quotations and extracts from well-known poets and writers, from Peter Pindar, Hume, Burke, Rousseau and Volney. The translation of the " Marseillaise " in Volume I, p. 67, of " Pigs' Meat," is similar to the one published in the *Newcastle Chronicle*, November 10, 1792. The pig that adorns some of his volumes as frontispiece bears a striking resemblance to the picture of a wonderful performing pig in the *Newcastle Chronicle*, July 27, 1787.

Many of the extracts in the papers are from books or articles by travellers and missionaries. Spence has much to say on the subject of Greenlanders, Red Indians and missionaries.

According to these volumes; he had read :—

Sir Thomas More : " Utopia."
Swift : " Sermons." " Gulliver's Travels."
Voltaire : " Philosophical Dictionary " (translation). " Candide."

Barlow : " Advice to the Privileged Orders."
Godwin : " Political Justice " (probably only in extracts).
Dyer : " Complaint of the Poor People in England," and
     Poems.
Volney : " Les Ruines " (translation).
Murray : Sermons.
J. L. Buchanan : " Travels in the Western Hebrides.'
Lord Lyttleton : " Letters from a Persian in England to
     his Friend in Ispahan."
Ogilvie : " Right of Property in Land." [1]

Then there are various pamphlets :—

William Freud : ' Peace and Union."
" A Tour through the Theatre of War in the Months of
     November and December 1792 and January 1793 "
     (Anon.). " Sins of the Nation " (Anon.).
Grant : " Peace and Reform."
" A Modest Plea for a Commonwealth " (1659) (Anon.).
Erskine's " Defence of Paine " (Gurney's edition of the trial).
Articles on press-gangs, duties of juries, etc.

He had certainly read some history, as his long
extracts from Roman, Swiss and Neapolitan history
show. He quotes voluminously from Nathaniel
Hooke's " Roman History," choosing such topics as
the expulsion of the kings and the secession of the
Plebs. Hooke's volumes were published 1738–71.
The " History of Masaniello," which he relates at
length, was published in Newcastle in 1768, price
1s. 6d. Masaniello was a fisherman who usurped the
Government of Naples for a few hours, but ruined
himself by his arrogance and folly.

Goldsmith's " A Citizen of the World " must also
be included as forming part of his historical reading.

---

[1] Ogilvie's " Essay " was published in 1781, but Spence probably
read it about 1793. He draws attention to it in a special note,
" Pigs' Meat," ii, p. 166.

He had read " Robinson Crusoe " and a dissertation on language by Sheridan. In his London publications he says that he had read Paine's " Rights of Man " and Charles Hall's essay on the " Effects of Civilization." Perhaps Locke's essay on " Government " ought to be included in the list.

" Locke's essay on ' Government ' and many other eminent works as well as the Bible have contributed to strengthen my confidence in this my millennial form of government, and therefore such books ought in justice to stand or fall with mine. ' Whether we consider natural reason (says Locke), which tells us that men once being born have a right to their Preservation and consequently to meat and drink, and such other things as Nature affords for their subsistence, or Revelation which gives an account of those grants of the world God made to Adam and to Noah and his sons, it is very clear that God, as King David says, Psa. cxv. 16, has given the earth to the children of men, given it to mankind in common ! ' . . . upon this Rock of Nature have I built my commonwealth and the gates of Hell shall not prevail against it." [1] He quotes in a similar fashion from Puffendorf's " Whole Duty of Man."

It would seem, from this, either that he had simply been reading extracts from these writers, or that he had read their books without fully understanding their meaning, and had fastened upon odd passages which

[1] " Important Trial," 1803, p. 59. In his " Interesting Conversation," " Rights of Man," 1793, p. 23, after reciting passages from Leviticus xxv., he says, " Well, we have heard what God has said on the subject, let us next hear what man says. " " Man " is Locke, and the passage quoted is the same as in his " Trial."

he had detached from their proper context and fitted into his own thought.

The list of books is meagre, but it is sufficient to show that Spence's mind was much occupied with projects of political reform and with criticism of the Government.

There is, however, one writer who had a real influence upon Spence, and he is James Harrington. There are more portions selected from his writings in " Pigs' Meat " than from the writings of anyone else. Spence remarks that he extracted " a valuable collection of general political principles, or fundamental truths in government " from Harrington's " Oceana " and his other works. " Portions of this collection will be frequently inserted in the course of this publication." [1] He quoted from the " Political Aphorisms " as well as from the " Oceana." He read long extracts to the unfortunate jury when he was being tried in 1801.

Traces of Harrington's influence may be observed in Spence's keenness for the ballot, in his belief that voters should have a property-qualification, and that Members of Parliament should be paid. He has, also, adopted Harrington's critical attitude to the Old Testament.

Harrington believed that society could only be secure and well organized if a proper balance of forces were maintained. This balance could be achieved if political powers were well distributed in the State, and this distribution could be accomplished if property were not too unequally divided amongst the different

[1] " Pigs' Meat," i, p. 79.

sections of the community. " All power in a State is of two sorts, external and internal, deriving from wealth on the one hand and from intellectual distinction on the other." [1] The better distribution of wealth could be secured if the quantity of land held by an individual was limited to what would yield £2,000 a year, and if primogeniture were abolished.

" Though he thought and wrote in terms of land, he realized that in commercial communities, such as Holland or Genoa, power would follow the distribution of capital." [2]

It is significant that Spence, in planning a regeneration of society, evolved a scheme in which a redistribution of land formed an essential part. The trend of Harrington's thought was political. Spence's thought was economic. This was due to the difference of the age in which each lived. In Harrington's time the general trend of thought was political ; in Spence's, physiocratic doctrines were rife, and men's thoughts naturally turned to the land question in its economic aspect to find explanations or solutions of the social problems of their time.

There is nothing to indicate that Spence, like Hone,[3] had a real love of reading, or that, like Place, he fully appreciated the advantages of education; yet he realized the social advantages entailed by a correct pronunciation of English. He never talks of bookhunts, or explains his failure to learn more than one language. Place was a poor man, but he studied

---

[1] Gooch, " Political Thought," p. 113, H.U.L.
[2] Ibid., p. 114, H.U.L.
[3] Hackett, " Life of Hone."

grammar, French and some mathematics when he had insufficient money for food and clothes, and had to borrow books from a bookseller. Perhaps the fact that Spence had a more creative mind accounts for this.

Little is known of Spence's religious beliefs, though Mackenzie leads one to suppose that the family attended the chapel of the Rev. J. Murray. Thomas Evans, the friend and biographer of Spence, says that the latter was a disciple of Murray. As Spence was always quoting from his publications, and as the Rev. J. Murray came to his assistance when he was in trouble, Evans would seem to be correct.

Mr. Murray was a Presbyterian minister. He had not been ordained by the Presbytery, as he believed in the Congregational system of Church government. His family had been persecuted as Covenanters, hence he disliked oppression and hated the Church of England. High Bridge Street Meeting House was built for him in 1765. Mackenzie says that, apart from his religion, he was cheerful, playful and facetious. He was independent and generous. He gave his second coat to a poor man whom he met out in the rain, and when he saw a Scotch drover, who had come late into chapel, standing because no one troubled to show him into a pew, he stopped his sermon and ordered that the drover should be shown into one immediately, saying that twenty pews would have been opened if he had had a fine coat and a powdered wig.

If the religious beliefs and practices of Jeremiah, the younger brother of Thomas, are considered in relation to the visions and political activities of the latter, it seems safe to conclude that the Spence family tried to follow Mr. Murray's example and to obey literally the injunctions of the Scriptures.

Mackenzie describes the sect of Glassites which worshipped at Forster Street Meeting House. This small community of dissenters existed for seventy years. "Among its most zealous members were . . . and Mr. Jeremiah Spence, slop-seller,[1] a man of the most distinguished worth. He and a few others who had belonged to the Rev. J. Murray's congregation joined the Glassites as being the most exempted from what they conceived to be the unscriptural aristocracy of religion." The most complete republican equality existed in their communities. They administered the Lord's Supper weekly, and dined together every Sabbath. They used the "kiss of charity," washed one another's feet, abstained from blood, and from eating anything that had been strangled. They believed in a community of goods up to a certain point; their possessions were, if necessary, to be used for the support of the poor of the chapel. Their ministers were generally tradesmen.[2]

Thomas Spence wished to revolutionize political society so that the Kingdom of God upon earth might be established. Jeremiah and his friends actually "revolutionized" their small religious society and made it conform to their conceptions of early Christian gatherings.

---

[1] Slop—Saloup—Saloop, a drink made from sassafras bark, see Lamb's Essays, "The Praise of Chimney Sweepers."

[2] Mackenzie, "History," i, p. 399 and notes.

Spence never mentions any of his relatives but his father and his son. His reminiscences of his father, and his concern at his parents' poverty, show his affection. Jeremiah was his friend and admirer. One of his sisters married a Mr. Joseph Glendinning, a Newcastle tailor. She had previously been married to a Mr. Gibson. Her son, John Gibson, died in Liverpool, January 20, 1810. He was a promising young man, who composed some songs " of considerable merit " which appeared in the " Northern Minstrel " and in " Northern Rhymes." [1]

According to Mackenzie, Spence first learnt his father's trade, then he became a clerk to a Mr. Hedley, a respectable smith. Later he opened a school of his own in Peacock's Entry on the Quayside. He taught in St. Ann's School, and for a short time had an engagement at Haydon Bridge Grammar School.[2]

If Mackenzie's brief sketch is accurate, it summarizes a real achievement.[3] No doubt little in the way of scholastic qualifications was demanded of teachers, and men often became schoolmasters because they were good for nothing else; yet Spence must have had some attainments or he would not have obtained a post both in St. Ann's School and in the Royal Free Grammar School. One hundred children

[1] Mackenzie, " Memoir," p. 10.
[2] Bewick, " Memoirs," p. 71, note, says, that Spence taught a school at the Broad Garth, Newcastle, afterwards writing and arithmetic in the Great School at Haydon Bridge, and lastly he was Master of St Ann's Public School, Sandgate. Peacock's Chare and Broad Garth were two of the twenty Chares leading from the Quay.
[3] Mitchell, *Newcastle Magazine*, January 1821 (Place, 27808, p. 303), says that Spence was also a market gardener, but there is no corroboration of this.

learnt reading and writing at St. Ann's School for
8d. a month. They paid 6d. extra to learn arithmetic.
The Writing Master was paid £20 per annum by the
corporation and also twenty guineas for other duties
and expenses. The usher had for salary house-rent,
coal and sixteen guineas for teaching psalmody.
Spence calls himself " Teacher of English in St. Ann's
School," so probably he was an extra member of the
staff.[1]

While he was at Haydon Bridge Spence married
a Miss Elliott of Hexham. This must have been
about 1781 or 1782, as he was then living in a house
of his own.[2] His son W—— was born somewhere
about this time. Marriage did not bring happiness
to Spence. He was "unfortunate" in his choice of a
wife.

He was not only beginning to make his way in the
world, he was also proving himself an original thinker.
Naturally his thought developed itself along the lines
of his own experience, an experience that had bred in
him a desire to help mankind. He wanted to remove
from the paths of his fellows thorns like those that had
beset his own. He himself traces the early development of his thought.[3] As a child he was oppressed
with a sense of injustice. He could not understand
why his parents should toil so hard and be so poor,
whilst others who did not deserve it had plenty.

" The contempt and ungenerous rebuffs of the

[1] Mackenzie, " History," ii, p. 451. Spence, advertisement in
Newcastle Courant, Saturday, January 12, 1782. (Below, p. 51.)

[2] Vide advertisement below, p. 51.

[3] Vide his " Interesting Conversation " published with the
Lecture, 1793, and his " Important Trial." Also Place, Add:
MSS. 27808, p. 154.

opulent I have already pretty well experienced and do yet expect, but the feelings occasioned by beholding the struggles of temperance, frugality and industry after an honest livelihood which ought to be easily attainable by everyone, have always been sufficiently powerful to enable me to despise them. Yes, those sympathetic feelings were impressed deep on my heart, being first excited by the many difficulties my poor parents met with in providing for, and endeavouring to bring up their numerous family decently and creditably, which I thought very hard, as none could be more temperate, frugal, nor industrious." [1]

He beheld some, too, who were in worse poverty than his own family.

His first reflections were centred on his father's lessons from the Bible. He had contrasted the Bible's promises with the actual state of society. Then he had come to reflect on societies in which there was, apparently, greater justice. Red Indians and Greenlanders had less unequal lots than the people of civilized nations. They were able to procure subsistence of a kind by hunting. " Savages may sometimes suffer through want, though that is but rare, but the poor tame wretch drags on in despicable miserable and toilsome existence from generation to generation." [2] He learned, too, from the Bible that there were the same injustices in the Jewish society as in the English. Moses had tried to solve the question by dividing out the land among the tribes and families and by ordaining a Jubilee Day when slaves should be freed and alienated lands should

[1] " Interesting Conversation," p. 33.   [2] Ibid., p. 30.

revert to their former owners.[1]   This seemed a childish
arrangement in Spence's eyes.   He looked forward to
the future as depicted by the prophets, when every
man should sit under his own vine and fig-tree.   That
future was impossible unless society had a new basis.
The Jewish and all other communities were transitory
because of a "mixture of injustice in the original
composition."[2]   The Jews, for instance, could hold
their fellows as slaves and deprive free men of their
share of land.   As he disliked the unfairness of Moses's
system, he decided to make a better, "unhampered
with the childish, narrow divisions of tribes and
families and other nurses of hereditary pride."

His reading and his religion both played their part
in shaping his thought and helping him to form his
Plan. A quarrel between the Corporation of Newcastle and the freemen over the Town Moor, in 1771,
seems to have made a great impression upon him.
The Corporation attempted to let 89 acres of this
Moor—where once had stood a fine oak forest which
had provided timber for the citizens' ships and houses—
to builders without consulting the freemen.   The
latter claimed that the land and the rents from the
land belonged to them and were at their disposal.
A lawsuit ensued, and the freemen won their case.
The townspeople were jubilant over this victory, and
illuminated their houses in honour of the occasion.
The excitement was evidently keen, for even the
anniversary of the victory was celebrated.   To-day
the Newcastle Races are run on the Town's Moor.
The contest must have filled Spence with a sense of

[1] See Leviticus xxv.   [2] "Important Trial," p. 57.

the importance of landed property, and he must have been struck with the injustice perpetrated by the magistrates in usurping rights over land that was town property.[1]

" Now I took a lesson from this affair which I shall never forget . . . the overbearing power of great men by their revenue and Samson by his hair are strikingly similar and show such men to be dangerous companions in society till scalped of their hair or revenues, for it is plain that the lords of the Philistines, if they had scalped Samson instead of only shaving him, they might have saved both their lives and their temple." [2]

He was thus led to think out the means by which the worst evils of society could, as he supposed, be counteracted. He sums the matter up with characteristic simplicity.

" When I first began to study, I found every art and science a perfect whole. Nothing was in anarchy but language and politics. But both of these I reduced to order, the one by a new alphabet the o_her by a new Constitution." [3]

[1] The freemen were only a small section of the population, but ultimately their victory was the town's.
[2] " Important Trial," p. 27.   [3] Ibid., p. 59.

CHAPTER II

A NEW ALPHABET AND A NEW CONSTITUTION

SPENCE published his supposed remedies, the " new alphabet " and the " new constitution," in the same year, 1775. The alphabet must have had precedence, as the new constitution was not published until after November 8, 1775. Spence's activities as an English teacher would probably lead him to grapple first with the alphabet.

Unfortunately, little is known of Spence at this period, but it is clear that he was winning recognition. His new constitution was the beginning of his misfortunes, so the recognition must have been due to his strength of character and to the originality of his ideas as displayed in the " new alphabet."

Assuming the priority of the alphabet, though the constitution may have been developed earlier in his own mind, it is possible to write a history of Spence that accords with his later history, for which there is more evidence.

His new alphabet was phonetic. He was anxious to make the learning of English easy and pleasant, to have " Ese Lesings fir Krusonein Skolirz." The object of the invention was not to improve the system of teaching, but to make it possible for people of every grade and class to acquire a good pronunciation. Thus social barriers between the classes would be removed. " Why should people be laughed at all their lives for betraying their vulgar education [1] when the evil is so easily remedied ? " The remedying of this evil would remove one of the worst curses of poverty.

THE NEW ALPHABET

Capitals.	Small Letters.	Names.
A	a	ā as in mane (MAN)
Λ	ă	ă as in man (MAN)
Λ	â	â as in father (FATHIR)
AJ	au	au as in wall (WAJL)
B	b	ib or bĭ
D	d	id or dĭ
E	ē	e as in meet
E	ĕ	ĕ as in met (MET)
F	f	f
G	g	ig or guĭ
H	h	hă
I	i	ī as in site (SIT)
Ɨ	ĭ	ĭ as in sit (SĬT)
J	j	idge or jĭ
K	k	ik or kĭ
L	l	il
M	m	im
N	n	in
O	o	ō as in note (NOT)
C	ŏ	ŏ as in not (NCT)
P	p	p or pĭ
R	r	ir
S	s	iss
T	t	it or ti
U	u	u as in tune (TUN)
Ʊ	ŭ	ŭ as in tun (TUN)
V	v	iv

---

[1] Place, 27808, p. 287. " Giant-Killer," No. 1, 1814.

Capitals.	Small Letters.	Names.
W	w	wĭ
Y	y	y as in young (YCNG)
Z	z	z
OO	oo	oo as in moon (MOON)
CI	oi	oi as in oil (OIL)
OJ	ou	ou as in house (H S)
SH	sh	sh as in shell
ƻH	zh	izh as in vision
CH	ch	itch as in child
TH	h	ith as in think
TH	th	ith as in they
WH	wh	whi as in which
NG	ng	ing as in living

∴ The vowels in this alphabet are A a, ⅄ a, Λ a, AJ, au, E e, E e, I i, Ɨi, O O, C o, U u, C o, OO, oo, CI oi, OJ ou; and the consonants L l, M m, N n, P p, R r, S s, T t, U u, W w, Y y, Z z, SH sh, ƻH zh, CH ch, H h, TH th, WH wh, NG ng.

In reading what is printed in this alphabet nothing is required but to sound every letter and but one way; for each letter represents but one sound, and that invariable in whatever position.

He published various pamphlets in which he made use of this new system. The " Grand Repository of the English Language . . . intended for the use of everyone whether native or foreigner that would acquire a complete knowledge of the English Language with the least waste of time and expense, but especially for those who are but indifferent Readers from not having been taught to pronounce properly" was printed by " T. Saint, for the Author and sold by him at his School on the Keyside, and by all the Booksellers in Town and County." It contained a " concise and comprehensive English Grammar with exercises of Bad English to be rectified by Rules of Syntax," the New Alphabet and " An Accurate New Spelling and Pronouncing English Dictionary."

In his Preface Spence refers to the proposals for publishing his work, and justifies it by quoting from " Mr. Sheridan's Dissertation on Language." He points out that the establishment of his alphabet will not mean that books in the old spelling will not be read. Publishers would suffer no more from the invention than from any new edition of books. If the public would support the undertaking, a weekly miscellany could be printed—a Bible could be printed in this spelling if there were a sufficient number of subscribers. It would be useful for the " laborious " part of the people who could only teach their children to read and write.

An advertisement in the " Grand Repository " announces that the author has just published " The Repository of Common Sense and Innocent Amuse- ment." It was sold by him " at his school on the Keyside and by the Booksellers and News-carriers." It cost one penny, and was to be continued weekly if a " competent number of subscribers is obtained," and will be delivered by the news-carriers (" to those who chuse to take it in ") in the same manner as any other weekly paper. The paper was to contain extracts from the " best authors in which every word is spelled according to the best pronunciation by the new alphabet." Subscriptions from those who can only afford one penny per week are invited.

Another small volume was published in 1782, " The Real Reading Made Easy."

What's this I read above is't possible
Such folk to teach, is't not a kind of miracle.
The barrier has been found so formidable
Few foreigners to surmount it have been able,
Then little book if thou this Fence throw'st down
And learning renderest common, twill work thy great renown.

The book cost one shilling, and consisted of extracts from the Scriptures—

> Ese Lesings fir Krusonein Skolirz.
> The'r Lord he iz the God.

His " S'upl'mint too thĭ Hĭstĭre ŏv Robinsin Kruzo " appeared the same year. It was published with another tract, " Progrēs ŏv Lirning in Lilipŭt," and with proposals for printing the Bible in the same manner. An edition of these tracts in ordinary spelling was issued. This was illustrated with wood-cuts. Two other tracts were included with it, " The History of the Marcolians " and " An Account of what Passed on a Journey with Old Zigzag "—on " tenderness to animals."

In his Preface Spence states that he wants to save foreigners and ordinary readers, the poor, industrious and innocent especially, from " vexation, tedium and ridiculous absurdities." He hopes that if his phonetics are used, charity schools will be unnecessary.

A long poem on reading the History of Crusonia is included in both versions of the Supplement. It is dated " July 7th, 1781," and is signed " J. S." It is evidently an eulogy written by Spence's brother Jeremiah.

The pamphlets must have interested those who came across them. Mackenzie says that when Spence was publishing the " Grand Repository . . ." he called on the Rev. Hugh Moises, Headmaster of the Grammar School and Morning Lecturer at All Saints', to ask him to be a subscriber. Spence had a strong north-country accent, and Mr. Moises asked him what opportunity he had had of acquiring a correct knowledge of English pronunciation.

" Pardon me," said Spence, " I attend All Saints' Church every Sunday morning ! " [1]

Perhaps Spence owed his engagement at Haydon Bridge to this interview !

Spence's publisher was Mr. T. Saint, editor of the *Newcastle Courant*, whose printing office was in Pilgrim Street. He was a brother of Mr. Joseph Saint, one of the proprietors of the Newcastle Bank, a common councillor, and treasurer to the infirmary.

It is reasonable to suppose that the " Newbery of Newcastle " [2] was interested in Spence and in the new line of children's books he had inaugurated.

Thomas Bewick, later the famous wood-engraver, was a personal friend of Spence. He calls him " one of the warmest philanthropists in the world," and says that " the happiness of mankind with him seemed to absorb his every consideration." He first met Spence in the workshops of the Greys, bookbinders.

" I cut the steel punches for Spence's types, and my Master (Bielby the engraver) struck them on the Matrices for casting his newly invented letters of the alphabet." [3]

---

[1] Mackenzie, "Memoir," p. 5.
[2] As the " Dictionary of National Biography " calls Saint in its article on Thomas Bewick. He was one of Bewick's first patrons. The latter illustrated children's books for him.
[3] Bewick, " Memoirs," pp. 71 and 73.

The alphabet had thus brought about this acquaint-anceship. Bewick gave a little account of Spence in his "Memoirs," besides supplying the editor of the *Newcastle Magazine* with material for an article on him. He handed over to the editor his own copy of "Pigs' Meat."

It is significant that Spence should have attracted the attention of Moises, Saint and Murray, all men of reputation in their day, and that he should have made a friend of Bewick.

He could find sympathizers, too, among the younger generation that was growing up. Æneas Mackenzie, the biographer of Spence, had lived in Newcastle since he was three years old. His family, like the Spence family, had come from Aberdeen. They had settled in Newcastle in 1781. Æneas seems to have known Spence personally and to have been the friend of Jeremiah. Perhaps he was a pupil of Thomas. He evidently admired him, for he published a special Memoir of him (in 1826) and included the Memoir in his "History of Newcastle" (1827). His father was a shoemaker. He himself began life as a shoemaker, then he became a Baptist minister, and after that a printer and publisher. The building of a Mechanics' Institute in Newcastle was partly due to him. He was one of the leaders in the agitation for parliamentary reform after 1819.[1]

To Spence, at twenty-five, life must have teemed with promise. He was launched on a career, he had

[1] Sykes, "Newcastle," ii, p. 342. Mackenzie published, amongst other things, a "View of the County of Northumberland," and "An Historical and Descriptive Account of Newcastle-upon-Tyne."

the companionship of young, talented men, and he could claim acquaintance with older men of note and position. His thought was developing, and he was finding the means to express it.

Mackenzie's description must apply to this happier period of his life.

" He had an open and expressive countenance, great liveliness of temper, and manners peculiarly affable and pleasing. In conversation he displayed much mildness and humour and was remarkably exempt from the sourness of political dogmatism." [1]

Bewick does not wholly corroborate this account.

" He was of a cheerful disposition, warm in his attachment to his friends and in his patriotism to his country ; but he was violent against people whom he considered of an opposite character, with such he kept no bounds." [2]

The representation of Spence's head upon his tokens shows a long, straight nose and pronounced chin. There are lines of humour about his mouth. His eyes are of the downward piercing type that can gleam with humour or blaze with fanaticism.

In 1775 the war with America began, and educated people found plenty of matter for debate in the causes of the quarrel. The Rev. J. Murray was one of the Newcastle townsmen who took up their pens. He wrote against the war, and answered Wesley's pamphlet which urged that taxation was no tyranny. The prerogative of rulers and the rights of man were fashionable topics. It is not surprising,

[1] " Memoir," pp. 9, 10.
[2] Bewick, " Memoir," p. 71.

therefore, that Spence should have dreamt of ending poverty by a new Constitution. Such ideas were in the air.

The times gave fresh zest to debating societies, and in 1775 a Philosophical Society was founded by some Newcastle gentlemen. The Rev. J. Murray seems to have been a member, also Sir M. W. Ridley, Bart. (later M.P. for Newcastle),[1] and other gentlemen of position. Mr. Chapman the engineer and Mr. Robert Doubleday were members. Another was a " gentleman equally well known for his literary ability and for his excellent and amiable character." [2]

Spence also joined the Society. It was the great opportunity of his life. Here was his chance to make friends with men of wealth and culture whose countenance and support would have been invaluable to him as a political thinker and social reformer.[3]

[1] Sir M. W. Ridley told the House of Commons in 1817 that he was a member of the Society to which Spence had belonged. Bewick, " Memoirs," note, pp. 72–3, clearly distinguishes Spence's membership of the Philosophical Society from his membership of a Society formed by himself.

[2] Mitchell, *Necwastle Magazine* (Place, 27808, p. 303). From what is said by Sykes, Mackenzie, Mitchell, and Bewick, it is safe to conclude that this Society was the precursor of the present Literary and Philosophical Society, proposed in 1792, founded January 1793. Of this later Society, Mr. Robert Doubleday, " an eminent citizen," was one of the Committee. The Rev. Edward Moises, relative and successor of the Rev. Hugh Moises, was a member, as were also Sir M. W. Ridley, Bart., M.P., and W. Chapman, Esq., M.R.I.A., Civil Engineer (Mackenzie, " Newcastle," ii, p. 461).

The Society met in Westgate Street (Mackenzie, i, p. 400). Strangely enough a Mr. Spence was librarian ! The gentleman " known for his literary ability," etc., supplied Mitchell with the rules of the older Society.—*Newcastle Magazine* (Place, 27808, p. 303). The rules are in the March number.

[3] Robert Owen's life is parallel at some stages with that of Spence. As a young man in Manchester he became a member of a literary and philosophical society, and made friends who were of the greatest service to him in his career.

According to the rules, which were agreed to and printed in 1777, the Society met on Thursdays, one part at six o'clock and the other part at eight o'clock. A fine of sixpence for absence was imposed. The questions to be discussed were selected by ballot. A member could be expelled by a majority if a ballot were taken. Members were liable to expulsion for attempting to injure the Society by scandalous aspersions, for refusing to comply with the rules, or for outrageously violating good order and decorum.

From what Spence says, it seems that it was a rule of the Society for each of the members in turn to read a paper.[1] On November 8, 1775, it was Spence's turn to read. He expounded his new Constitution which was to redeem society.

The first part of the paper[2] is an answer to the question " whether mankind in society reap all the benefits from their natural and equal rights of property in land and liberty, which in that state they possibly may and ought to expect."

Spence begins by assuming that in a state of nature " property in land and liberty among men " were equal. The country of a people in their natural state may be regarded as their common. (Query : What is their " country " ?) To question their right to the products of the country is to question their right to

[1] 1793 edition of his lecture. Beer, reprint, p. 5. " Mr. President, it being my turn to lecture . . ."

[2] The first edition of the Lecture is not extant. That published in 1793, the " Rights of Man," and the subsequent version in 1795, vary so little from one another that it seems safe for the present purpose to act as though the 1793 and 1775 editions are identical. The 1796 edition has a fresh paragraph substituted for one of the concluding paragraphs ; it is an alteration that affects some details of the scheme. See Appendix, p. 250.

live. The people ought not to sell or to give away their land, as in so doing they are depriving their descendants of their means of subsistence and thus assuming the right to deprive them of life. " For the right to deprive anything of the means of living supposes a right to deprive it of life, and this right ancestors are not supposed to have over their posterity." Society is the mutual agreement among the inhabitants of a country to maintain the natural rights and privileges of one another (i.e. to maintain the right to life and hence the right to a means of subsistence). It is plain that the land or earth in any country or neighbourhood belongs at all times to the " living inhabitants of the said country or neighbourhood in an equal manner."

The land and its productions were originally claimed by a few individuals who acted as if it were a possession that they had manufactured for themselves. As no one disputed their right or called them to account, these individuals came to look upon themselves as lords, and to regard not only the land but all its appurtenances as their own property. Thus the lives of all the creatures, man and beast, really depended upon these lords, for by granting the means of life, they granted life itself. The first landlords were tyrants and usurpers. Those who have since possessed the land have done so by right of purchase and inheritance. Landlords make the laws and so have the power of turning every living creature off their property.

" Thus men may not live in any part of this world, not even where they are born, but as strangers."

They have to pay extravagantly for the permission, too. Landlords justify their position by likening themselves to manufacturers, and say that they should live by their business as well as they can.

Spence next proceeds to outline a scheme which will enable mankind to reap all the advantages possible from the " common gifts of nature," " liberty, air, or the light and heat of the sun " and " property in land."

This is the Plan.

Assume that a whole people agrees that every man has an equal property in the land of the neighbourhood where he resides. Assume also that people live together in society in order that they may reap the full benefits that they ought to expect.

Then, let the inhabitants of each parish meet on a fixed day to take possession of their long-lost rights and to form themselves into a corporation. Each corporation is to have the same power as a lord of the manor over his land and houses, and to be " sovereign lord of its own territories," though it is agreed " by the whole nation " that alienation shall not be allowed.[1]

The parish land will be rented in small lots to tenants who will bid for farms at a public auction. The rents paid for the land will be paid into the parish treasuries and will be used to pay the share of governmental expenses demanded by Parliament (? the central government), to maintain the poor of the parish, to pay the salaries of officials, and to provide the money necessary for local public works.

---

[1] Spence contradicts himself. If the corporation is sovereign lord, who is to prevent it alienating its land ? A lord of a manor is not a " sovereign lord."

As regards the government of the country, all affairs are to be settled by voting, which shall take place by ballot in full meetings of the parishes, in its committees, or in the " House of Representatives " (? Parliament). The Government is to allow the parishes to have full discretion in their enforcement of the laws of the country, and is only to interfere when a parish is manifestly acting to the prejudice of society.

Each member of Parliament represents a group of neighbouring parishes. The parishes each have an equal number of votes in the election, and each pays an equal share towards the maintenance of the member. Candidates will be nominated on the same day in every parish and elected by ballot on the same day.

A year's residence will qualify a man as a parishioner. He will remain a member of that parish until he has resided a full year in another parish, when he will automatically become a member of the new parish and the old membership will lapse. Foreigners and strangers from distant parishes who become chargeable to the parish in which they are residing will be maintained by that parish, but the expense will be refunded by the Exchequer.

All men in the parish are to be trained in the art of war so as to be able to defend their own property. If an army is required for offence it can be raised by volunteers from the parishes.

Land let in small farms makes employment for a greater number of hands and is productive of a greater quantity and variety of foods.[1] It will therefore be

---

[1] This is obviously fallacious.

let in small farms, because each man has a vote in all the affairs of his parish, and for his own sake he must wish well to the public.

Trade will be free, because rent paid for the land will cover all charges, national or local. " Freedom to do anything whatever cannot be bought, a thing is either entirely prohibited as theft or murder, or entirely free to everyone without tax or price." [1]

Rent will not be so high, because the Government will not require such a large host of officials as under the present system. It will employ just the necessary officials and at just a sufficient salary. Even if rents have to be raised in order to cover taxation, the saving effected by the new system will prevent the increase from being a burden. There will be no devouring landed interest to support. The taxes may just as well be paid in a lump sum as by instalments, and the Government will thus be saved inconvenience and expense. If only this new system is installed, the " Empire of Right and Reason will exist for Ever."

As his lecture was partly an attack on landlords, i.e. owners of private property in land, and as Spence was not guarded in his remarks, there is much in the lecture which might cause offence if he were not on exceptionally good terms with the members of the Society. In the light of what follows, it is plain that he could not have been popular. Perhaps he had offended his social superiors by bluntness and lack of deference.

[1] Lecture, 1793, p. 5.

He immediately printed his lecture—Davenport says [1] in accordance with the advice of Murray and his friends—and because of this, so he tells us, he was expelled from the Society.[2] Mackenzie's account of the affair is that he was expelled " not for printing it only, but for printing it in the manner of a halfpenny ballad and having it hawked about the streets." The *Newcastle Magazine* gives the same explanation.[3] The Society did not like " ignoble modes of circulation." (Mitchell says that Spence appears to have forgotten this fact.) Sir John E. Swinburne pointed out in a letter to the *Quarterly* [4] that Spence read his strange paper, which was " heard with very little attention," and published it as an Essay read at the Philosophical Society. For thus using the Society's name, a member moved that he should be expelled, and it was decided unanimously that he should.

" By outrageously violating good order and decorum," Spence had lost his opportunity of making friends who could have helped him.

Mr. Murray, as one would expect, came to his aid. He addressed the Society on his behalf by sending them a set of queries. He sent Spence a copy of these queries. On it is written :—

[1] Another friend and biographer. " Life," p. 3. He says that the title was " On the Mode of Administering the Landed Estate of the Nation as a Joint Stock Property in Parochial Partnerships by Dividing the Rent."

[2] Vide Spence, " Meridian Sun." Title-page.

[3] Mackenzie, " Memoir." Mitchell, *Newcastle Magazine*.

[4] " Southey Essays," 1832, vol. i, p. 97, " On the Rise and Progress of Popular Disaffection." The then (1817) President of the Society, Sir J. E. Swinburne, instructed his secretary to state this in a letter to the *Quarterly*. He wanted to dissociate *his* Society from that of Spence's time.

Received this from Mr. M——y December 23rd 1775. You will much oblige justice by returning pertinent answers to the above directed for him to the care of Mr. Thomas Bewick, Engraver with Mr. Bielby, Newcastle.

There are eighteen of these queries.

1. Whether according to the law of Nature anyone has a right to property in land.

4. " Do people act contrary to any divine law when they resume their rights and recover their property out of the hands of those who have unnaturally invaded it ? "

15. " May not poor people speak concerning their rights, though they have but little hope of obtaining them ? "

18. " Will it not take a great quantity of sophistry to answer these questions consistently with the principles of the Philosophic Society concerning the expulsion of Mr. Spence ? " [1]

Spence felt the rebuff keenly, as his publication of the queries in 1793 and his reference to the honour that the Society had paid him in expelling him testify. But by 1793 he had grown used to the rebuffs of the wealthy.[2]

So Spence was left to his teaching and his thinking. From this time he became more and more absorbed in his Plan.

Two incidents, narrated by Spence himself, show how full his thoughts were of the Plan and of subjects kindred to it.

[1] Place, Add. MSS., 27808, p. 235.
[2] The queries were published with the 1793 edition of the Lecture. See his remark to this effect in the " Interesting Conversation," p. 33, and above, p. 24.

About 1777 Spence was gathering nuts in a wood near Hexham. "While I was in the wood alone by myself agathering of nuts, the Forester popped through the bushes upon me to ask what I did there. I answered, gathering nuts. Gathering nuts, said he, and dare you say so? Yes, said I, why not? Would you question a monkey or a squirrel about such a business? And am I to be treated as inferior to one of those creatures? or have I a less right? But who are you, continued I, that thus take it upon you to interrupt me? I'll let you know that, said he, when I lay you fast for trespassing here. Indeed, answered I, but how can I trespass here where no man ever planted or cultivated? For these nuts are the spontaneous gifts of nature ordained alike for the sustinence of man and beast that chuse to gather them and therefore they are common. I tell you, said he, this wood is not common. It belongs to the Duke of Portland. Oh! my service to the Duke of Portland, said I. Nature knows no more of him than of me. Therefore as in Nature's store-house the rule is ' First come, first served,' so the Duke of Portland must look sharp if he wants any nuts."[1]

Where is the Englishman's privilege, Spence asked, if he may not pluck a nut? Was it for this that people were called upon to serve in the militia? As the forester allowed Spence to continue gathering the nuts, he must have enjoyed these humorous remonstrances.

In the summer of 1782 an old man, eighty years

[1] "Restorer," Letter V, p. 31. When writing in 1800 Spence said that this " sylvan joke " was three and twenty years old.

of age, and his wife made one of the caves at Marsden
Rocks near South Shields their place of residence.
The man had been a miner at Allenheads, but, having
removed to Shields to save the expenses of house-
keeping, the old couple decided to live in this cave,
which they furnished. The romance and novelty
drew a number of visitors to the cave. The couple
provided refreshments, and even ladies and gentlemen
drove to the place and partook of their cheer.[1] One
of the visitors was Spence. He describes how he went
to see the old miner who had been likewise a farmer
and had been ill-treated by his landlord.

Spence, " exulting in the idea of a human being
who had emancipated himself from the iron fangs of
aristocracy," wrote in chalk above the fire-place :—

> Ye landlords vile who man's peace mar
> Come levy rents here if you can,
> Your stewards and lawyers I defy
> And live with all the rights of Man.[2]

Spence was trying to make his Plan known by
every means in his power. During the years 1779–84
he was busy publishing tracts illustrative of his
alphabet and of his Constitution.

He published a tract called the " Poor Man's Advocate " in 1779. This contained " queries of importance." He asks whether one horse should usurp
all the pasture, whether a landless horse was not most
miserable, whether a horse who could show the others
a better way should be branded with " selfishness,

[1] Sykes, i, p. 321.
[2] " Pigs' Meat," iii, p. 250. Either Spence or Sykes must have
forgotten the exact date of this event. Sykes says 1782, Spence
" about " the year 1780.

levelling, turbulency, sedition, or other hard names,"
whether buying and selling land is as bad, according
to the law of nature, as stealing goods ?   Whether, if
trafficking in land is an incitement to industry, is not
trafficking in men ? [1]

Hone, writing to Place,[2] says that the only publications of Spence that he possesses he " deems the
rarest and most curious of his works."   These are the
" Real Reading Made Easy " and the " Supplement
to the History of Robinson Crusoe."   The modern
reader must endorse Hone's remarks.

The colonists of Crusoe's island, Crusonia, assemble
and decide that they will adopt the Crusonian system.

" We intend to have no Landlords but the Parishes
and to make every parish a corporation and every
man a parishioner and member of that Parish, and
that only he last dwelt a full year in, notwithstanding
what other Parish, County or Nation he might come
from prior to such settlement.   A small rent or rate
shall, according to the determination of the parishioners,
be paid by every Person, suitable to the valuation of
the Houses and Land he possesses, to the Parish
Treasury to be put to such uses as the majority please
and each parish shall have all the uncontrollable
Power that can possibly be made good use of by a
corporation, to be connected only by a Parliament
for the common strength and welfare of the whole."

The capital of the island is described.   " This town
is built on each side of a commodious harbour, a

---

[1] " Pigs' Meat," ii, pp. 32–35. From a pamphlet entitled
" The Poor Man's Advocate," published at Newcastle by T. Spence
in 1779.   There is no trace of this publication.
[2] Place, Add. MSS., 27808, p. 314.

considerable river falls into it, and at the upper end
of the harbour there is a most elegant bridge. The
town extends about a mile on each side along the shore
and half a mile outward towards the country, and contains about fifty thousand inhabitants. Four parishes
meet and have their churches in it, two on each side,
whose steeples are very magnificent and a great
ornament to the town. It is full of superb and well-
furnished shops and has every appearance of grandeur,
opulence and convenience one can conceive to be in
a large place flourishing with trade and manufacture."

This must surely be Newcastle idealized. Mr. Mann
and Captain Wishit, the visitors to this island, converse together on the advantages of the system.
They discuss landlordism, the evils of bribery and
open voting, the advantage of the ballot. The Captain
notes that all the Crusonians are trained as soldiers.
Each parish sees to the training of its members, but
the Parliament appoints the general. He attends a
military review. The beauty and order of the country
strike him. He sees no patched windows, no smoky
houses, nor broken pavements. He finds that agriculture is stimulated by the award of premiums, and
by the fact that the Crusonian system of leasing
means security for the lessee.

Strangers are encouraged to settle in Crusonia.
When the island becomes too crowded, the Crusonians
will spread to the Continent. The Parliament will
then appropriate land for each parish as required.
It will take no smaller piece of land than is necessary
for a parish.

The Parliament consists of three hundred members.

As there are only a few parishes, four or five members are returned from one parish. When the number increases, two or three parishes must join to elect one member. The parishes must draw lots for the privilege of electing any surplus M.P.'s. The parishes provide clothes and salaries for officials of the parish. The nation provides for national officials. The parishes are taxed according to their ability to pay.

There is a free school and a public library in each parish, and the best teachers are provided. Besides a school and a library, the parish has a theatre and assembly rooms. Crusonia has a National University.

The country is called the " United Parishes of Crusonia." Each parish is " as distinct and separate " as states can be of so small a size. Like other petty states, they must be united under one " guardian head to hinder them from altering their own constitutions and for mutual defence both against the injustices of one another and of greater societies."

There are local courts of justice. Though all religions are tolerated, the majority in each parish decides what religious establishment it will support. Instead of tithes, the preachers are paid salaries by the parish authorities.

The other publications in the " Supplement " have all some bearing on the Plan.

In the " Rise and Progress of Learning in Liliput " Spence shows how the use of the Crusonian alphabet leads to all the Liliputians becoming educated, and how education improves their manners and their customs. It led, for instance, to the abolition of landlords.

His " Jubilee Hymn " is really part of a play or

pageant which is to take place when the Crusonian system is established.

> Hark how the trumpets sound
> Proclaims the Land around
> The Jubilee.
> The Learning of Liliput
> Tells all the Poor oppressed
> No more shall they be cess'd
> Nor Landlords more molest
> Their Property.
>
> The Parish rate is all
> Paid now by great or small
> For House or Land,
> No more by Nature's due
> God gave this Earth to you
> And not unto a few
> But to all mankind.

" The History of the Marcolians " is a discourse on the subject of voting by ballot. He wants elections all to take place on the same day. The Marcolians have raised a Temple of Fame to celebrate all the trades.

Thomas Bewick told Mitchell " that he had many arguments with him (Spence) in which he strongly urged that if he wished to try his system he might go to some island and found a colony, but that in England the strenuous advocacy of such ideas was only calculated to unsettle men's minds without giving them any means of recovering from their dissatis-faction." Spence clung obstinately to his Plan, although he published a book in which he imagined Robinson Crusoe returning to his island to put his scheme into operation.[1]

According to Bewick himself, Spence " got a number

[1] Place, 27808, p. 303. *Newcastle Magazine*, January 1821.

of young men gathered together, and formed into a debating society which was held in the evenings in his schoolroom in the Broad Garth, Newcastle," for " the purpose chiefly of making converts to his opinion that property in land is everyone's right." Bewick attended some of these meetings. His description of one of them characterizes Spence and throws some light on his failure to win many friends or adherents. One night Spence's favourite project (i.e. the Plan) was to be debated. He counted upon Bewick's support, for the latter had tacitly assented to some of the Plan, though he did not think that the present state of society should be upset, and he " considered that property ought to be held sacred . . . that the honestly obtaining it was a great stimulus to industry. . . ." At the meeting the question was decided against Spence. Bewick had failed to defend him, so he vented his swelling indignation upon his friend, whom he challenged to a cudgelling match as he was not " stout enough " to thrash him. Bewick defeated him, and " he became quite outrageous and acted very unfairly, which obliged me to give him a severe beating." [1]

Spence's exertions were meeting with little success. He was failing even with his own friends and associates. He was " often heard to say that there was no scope for ability in a provincial town, and that London was the only place where a man of talent could display his powers." [2] His failure probably accounts for his irritability.

[1] Bewick, ' Memoir," pp. 72-3.
[2] Place, 27808, p. 303. *Newcastle Magazine*, January 1821, p. 316.

There is no trace of any publication of his between 1784 and 1792. His pamphlets cannot have sold well, and the expenses of publication may have left him out of pocket. Nor can his teaching have been highly successful. He did not hold the position at Haydon Bridge long. He says nothing of his teaching experience during these years, but his advertisement in the *Newcastle Courant* for January 12, 1782, provides one piece of autobiography.

Just published. Price Sixpence bound.

PRINTED AND SOLD BY T. SAINT,

A SUPPLEMENT TO
" ROBINSON CRUSOE,"

BEING THE HISTORY OF
CRUSONIA, OR ROBINSON CRUSOE'S ISLAND,
DOWN TO THE PRESENT TIME.

This book is printed and planned as to be the best adapted for a Reading Made Easy or First Book for teaching English upon at any time ever offered to the world, the transition from this book to others being also easy, as a proof of which Mr. Spence, Teacher of English in St. Ann's School, Newcastle, instructs on it with the greatest ease and pleasure to himself and scholars, not only children and grown persons of any age from their letters whose Mother-tongue is English, but Highlanders, Indians, Frenchmen, Dutchmen or foreigners of any nation or language, who would learn to speak or read English, and soon qualifies them to become as good teachers of their countrymen as himself. This he does at his school in the daytime, and at his house Head of the Side from 6 o'clock in the evening, and by the experiments he has made, he is so far certain of answering the highest expectations of success that he leaves his reward to be regulated according to the progress of his pupils.

From this advertisement it is legitimate to conclude that Spence had teaching engagements during the day and kept an evening school. He was clearly finding it difficult to attract pupils.

There is no indication that Spence had ever the moral support of his relatives during these years. Jeremiah remained faithful to him. They may have been simply indifferent, or ashamed and alarmed at his failure to maintain himself. Perhaps his declining fortune was the root cause of the unhappiness of his marriage. He was irritable himself, and the temper of the best of wives would have been sorely tried. It must have been hard for her to grow daily poorer because her husband was too engrossed in securing the happiness of mankind to keep his own family in comfort.

The last traces of Spence in Newcastle must be sought in the newspapers and directories of the years 1784–92. One of his pamphlets is advertised in the *Courant* of December 24, 1784,[1] and an advertisement in the *Newcastle Chronicle* for December 7, 1787, must be his, if it is judged by the style. Unfortunately, " Spence " is a common name in the north.

SPENCE'S REGISTRY OFFICE. HEAD OF THE PUDDING CHAIR (= Lane).

T. Spence respectfully informs the public that he transacts with integrity the business of a Register Office at his Toy-shop, Head of the Pudding Chair, where applications for men or maid-servants of any description will be punctually and diligently attended to.

N.B.—On account of the applications for servants at the above office, those servants who apply there and can be recommended may expect soon to be hired.

---

[1] *Courant*. Advertisement of " The Wonderful Life and Surprising Adventures of that renowned hero Robinson Crusoe, who lived twenty-eight years on an uninhabited island which he afterwards colonized." Price 6d. But perhaps this is just a cheap edition of " Robinson Crusoe."

Spence finally resolved to go to London. He does not say why nor precisely when he went. It is easy, however, to make sound conjectures as to his reasons for quitting Newcastle.

Mackenzie says that he went because he was unhappy at home and because he wanted to make his Plan better known. Evans says that after his expulsion from the Philosophical Society children were kept from his school.

A schoolmaster who taught his pupils to spell and write according to a system of phonetics used solely by himself, who found political panaceas that threatened private property, and who had pamphlets hawked in the streets, was not likely to keep his pupils. Perhaps he did not fare well at the hands of the latter. When Bell's system was introduced the discipline of St. Ann's School improved.[1] Evidently Spence showed no remarkable qualities as a disciplinarian. A tender-hearted crank would probably not make a good schoolmaster.

If the Registry Office advertisement is his, it is a proof that his teaching occupations were gone and that his new business was not prospering.

The Rev. J. Murray died in 1782 and Mr. Thomas Saint in 1788.[2] So Spence may have found himself at last almost friendless and penniless, with a number of indignant relatives who had looked to him for support and feared now lest he should become a burden.

---

[1] Mackenzie, " Newcastle." This comment on the discipline of St. Ann's School appeared in 1827. Mackenzie would surely have commented on the fact, if Spence's teaching had been particularly successful.

[2] Mackenzie, Sykes, and current newspapers.

But Jeremiah must have sympathized with his brother, and even have approved of his Plan. He struck some token-coins for Spence before he left Newcastle.

O. Spence's Glorious Plan is Parochial Partnership in Land without private Landlordism. Centre, within a radiated circle, " Spence's Plan, Nov. 8th, 1775."

R. Hand holding an olive branch. Below it are a pair of scales and a cornucopia. " This just plan will produce everlasting Peace and Happiness, in fact the Millennium." [1]

Perhaps Jeremiah was the link between his brother and Mackenzie.

There must also have been a strong bond of sympathy between Spence and his son, for the latter accompanied him to London, while Mrs. Spence remained behind in Newcastle and supported herself by keeping a shop.

By December 1792 Thomas Spence, full of hope that his Plan would be appreciated by the dwellers in the metropolis, was established in London.

[1] A. Waters, " Trial of T. Spence," p. 20.

CHAPTER III

THE PLAN IN LONDON

SPENCE'S hopefulness may be measured by the disappointment that he evinced later. Nevertheless, his hopes were not ill-founded. His chances of finding friends and sympathizers were much greater in London than in Newcastle. London, in the last ten years of the eighteenth century, was just the place for him.

The development of new industrial areas and the decay of the old were making parliamentary reform a necessity. The rapid progress of the Industrial Revolution in the latter part of the century was making the anomalies of the existing representative system more glaring. After 1769 a minority of the Whig opposition to the Government was demanding some measure of reform. In 1780 certain of its advocates, amongst whom were Fox and Burke, founded the Society for Promoting Constitutional Information. They hoped to stimulate public opinion by holding meetings and by distributing pamphlets.

An interest in politics was kindled by the American War and fanned by the Press. Magazines and newspapers were becoming more numerous and cheaper and were being circulated more widely.[1] In the big

[1] See Lecky and Spencer Walpole.

towns, and in London particularly, papers were available at the taverns for customers to read. Those who could not read could take part in the political discussions which were the order of the day. The greater freedom of the Press after 1771 [1] added zest to the diffusion of political information, and encouraged the increasing class of journalists and reporters.

The French Revolution provided a further stimulus. Such topics as the "Rights of Man" and the "Sovereignty of the People" became current talk.

A small band of enthusiasts, like Fox, Wordsworth, Coleridge, Southey, Paine, Dr. Price and the Revolutionary Society [2] hailed the French Revolution as the dawn of a new era. Burke, consistently with his philosophy, expressed his abhorrence of it as early as 1789. His attitude led to the quarrel with Fox. Those who welcomed the Revolution regarded him as a traitor, but his conservatism appealed to the majority of his countrymen. The course taken by the Revolution justified his attitude, and, later, when war broke out in 1793, sympathy with France came to be regarded as treachery.

In London, the political excitement had manifested itself in the renewed vigour of the Society for Promoting Constitutional Information, and in the formation of other societies which demanded parliamentary reform and supported Fox as against Burke. Associations of loyal citizens were likewise founded in opposition to these. One of the latter was formed

[1] From 1771 the publication of parliamentary debates was tacitly allowed.
[2] Founded to celebrate the Revolution of 1688.

in London as the outcome of a meeting at the " Crown and Anchor " Tavern in 1792. A Mr. Reeves was the chairman.

Of the former, the Society of Friends of the People, founded in 1792, and the London Corresponding Society, founded in 1791, were the best known.[1] The establishment of similar societies in other towns was partly due to the " missionary " zeal of the London societies. The London Corresponding Society, which was founded by Thomas Hardy, a shoemaker, and had as its object the diffusion of political information among the lower middle and labouring classes, made a special point of missionary work.

Many members of these societies wanted such radical reforms as universal suffrage, voting by ballot, and annual parliaments. Those who were more under French influence were republicans. In their enthusiasm for the Revolution, the Society of Friends of the People and the London Corresponding Society sent congratulatory addresses to the French revolutionary leaders.

The Government adopted a repressive attitude towards these societies. The inefficiency of the police system made the danger of riots originating with the unemployed and criminal classes much greater than it is to-day, and in the latter part of the eighteenth

[1] The first meeting of the London Corresponding Society was on January 25, 1792. Subscription 1d. per week and 1s. entrance fee. Place gives a full account of these societies, 27808, p. 1. The subscription to the Constitutional Society was £5 5s. per annum and £1 1s. entrance fee. The subscription to the Friends of the People was 2½ guineas per annum and 2½ guineas on election.

century this danger was more acute because the population was increasing rapidly and food was scarce. The memory of the Gordon Riots in 1780 and the results of mob-rule in France made the authorities vigilant. They were distrustful of societies and of agitators who were considered to have a disturbing influence on the minds of the lower orders.

In London, then, Spence could be more in touch with the most advanced reformers. He would have a better opportunity for hearing for himself the most recent political opinions and of finding expression for his own. The London Corresponding Society could give him more scope than the Newcastle Philosophical Society. His chance of finding friends who would at least tolerate his opinions was greater. It was his misfortune to have been born in Newcastle. He was out of place in an old-established and prosperous seaport. He should have been born in London or among the underpaid workers herded in slums round Manchester, Sheffield, or Birmingham, though in any of these places he might have suffered more from the oppression of authorities than he did in London. Even in London it behoved him to proceed with great caution if he meant to steer clear of the authorities.

Spence must have left Newcastle some time in November 1792.[1] At any rate, he was settled in London by December 6th of that year, for he was then keeping a saloop and bookstall at the Eastern

---

[1] The version of the " Marseillaise " in " Pigs' Meat " was published in the *Newcastle Chronicle*, November 10, 1792. So Spence may have been in Newcastle then.

Corner of Chancery Lane and Holborn.[1]   His landlord
was a Mr. John Harrington, a trunk-maker.   Place,
who knew Spence when he had this stall, says that
it was formed by a shallow bulk along the wall, and
that it projected one foot upon the pavement, which
was only four feet wide.   Such bulks were common
in London streets, in the Strand, for instance, in
front of houses and shop windows.

Place describes Spence as well as his stall.   " He
. . . was querulous in his disposition and odd in his
manners, he was remarkably irritable and seemed as
if he had always been so, his disposition was strongly
marked in his countenance, which marked him as a
man soured by adverse circumstances and at enmity
with the world. . . .   In person he was short, not
more [than] five feet high, he was small and had the
appearance of feebleness at an age when most men
still retain their vigour, this was however partly
occasioned by a stroke of palsy from which he never
entirely recovered.   His face was thin and much
wrinkled, his mouth was large and uneven, he had a
strong northern ' burr ' in his throat and a slight
impediment in his speech.   His garments were generally
old and sometimes ragged . . . he had not, therefore,
many points of attraction." [2]

This description differs from that of Mackenzie, but

---

[1] Place first knew him when he was keeping this stall.   He had
not therefore been long in London.

[2] Place, 27808, pp. 152-154.   Professor Graham Wallas quotes
this description in his " Life of Francis Place," p. 60 : " Case of
T. Spence . . . 1793."   " Here the reader ought to be informed
that Mr. Spence some time since (i.e. before 1792) had a stroke
of palsy which has rendered his frame somewhat feeble and of
course less like to withstand experiments."

the discrepancy is easily reconciled. Both Mackenzie and Place are writing some years after Spence's death. Mackenzie, fourteen years old at most when Spence left Newcastle, is depending on his youthful recollections or on the recollections of those who had known Spence in happier days. Place is summing up the general impression made by Spence when misfortune had already soured him, when he was in extreme poverty, and when he had recently recovered from an illness that would age him, make him irritable, and account for the impediment in his speech. Perhaps Bewick's description, which is more in agreement with Place's, marks the transition from cheery excitable youth to disappointed middle-age. Place says of him also that "he was a very simple, very honest, single-minded man." Though "soured by adverse circumstances," yet "he loved mankind and firmly believed that the time would come when it would be wise, virtuous and happy."

"He was perfectly sincere, unpractised in the ways of the world to an extent few could imagine in a man who had been pushed about in it as he had been. Yet what is still more remarkable, his character never changed, and he died as much of a child in some respects as he probably was when he arrived at the usual age of mankind." He had a firm belief in his scheme and a great contempt for those who disagreed with him. He was apt to be offensive when opposed. He could not compromise, and would not have dreamt of concealing his opinions. He thought that his scheme was so good that those who differed from him must do so from dishonesty. He was excitable and lacked friends who could have helped him materially. He was contemptuous of the ordinary man, thought him a despicable willing slave, and told him so. He " expected his reward in the honour men would bestow upon his memory." He was endured rather than tolerated by men whose circumstances were above his own, but those who knew him better appreciated his social qualities.[1]

Spence threw himself vigorously into the political turmoil of the day in the hope of giving effect to his Plan. He sold Reform literature—Tom Paine's " Rights of Man "—he associated himself with the London Corresponding Society and became acquainted with certain of its members—Alexander Galloway, Thomas Evans, Francis Place. He kept a petition for peace at his shop and invited signatures to it on one of his broadsheets.[2]

But his Plan absorbed his chief energy. He was always advertising it, by chalk and charcoal notices on walls and public places, by disputes and argumentations, by the sale or distribution of handbills and broadsheets, by a constant output of tracts and pamphlets. A glance at the list of his publications from 1792–1801 will show what time and activity he devoted to the cause. He tried to enlist the services of friends, and he trained his son as his assistant.

He followed the established custom of issuing a cheap periodical. His first and most famous was " Pigs' Meat " (1793–96), a penny weekly, deriving its

---

[1] Place, 27808, p. 152, and Professor Graham Wallas, p. 60.
[2] Vide Appendix, p. 218–19, 246–47.

title from Burke's famous allusion to the " swinish multitude." The numbers were afterwards collected and sold in volume form. A few articles are anonymous, and a few are by Spence himself; but the majority are extracts from well-known authors and poets. The extracts selected are such as would, in the opinion of the author, provide suitable nourishment for the swinish multitude.

At the end of Part I, Volume II, of " Pigs' Meat," Spence advertises that he is about to publish a new penny weekly, " Eye-Salve." Nothing more is known of this, so probably he abandoned his intention. His next weekly publication was the " Giant-Killer or Anti-Landlord," which appeared in 1814.[1]

Spence wrote verse as well as prose. Most of his publications have odd verses interspersed amongst them. Some are in " Pigs' Meat." Some were published separately. They were also collected and published in tract form (1803, 1807) together with the effusions of certain disciples. They generally have some bearing on his scheme, either by way of laudation or explanation, and are modelled after well-known songs and ballads, " God Save the King," " Chevy Chase," " Rule Britannia," " Babes in the Wood." About 1793 he began to circulate his " Rights of Man in Verse," which he said was first published in 1783.

A few samples from his own favourites must suffice to illustrate Spence's powers as a verse-writer.

---

[1] Vide Appendix, pp. 235, 242, for a more detailed description of these publications. Two numbers of the " Giant-Killer " are preserved by Place, Add. MSS., 27808, p. 233.

"Jubilee Hymn," verse 3. (1782.)

How hath the oppressor ceas'd
And all the world released
From misery.
The Fir Trees all rejoice
And Cedars lift their voice,
Ceas'd now the Fellers' noise
Long raised by thee.

"Rights of Man in Verse." (1783.)

Man nothing less than lord was made
For nothing less was meant,
That all things else he should subdue
He to this world was sent.

.   .   .   .

But not content with this large sway
Their brethren men subdue,
And all the godlike race is made
Subservient to a few.

.   .   .   .   .

If grass or nettles we could eat
The same would be deny'd,
For my lord's land and herbage reach
Close to the highway side.

Southey quotes an epilogue of his which he calls
" decent verse."

The Golden Age, so fam'd by Men of Yore,
Shall soon be counted fabulous no more.

.   .   .   .   .   .

Yes, all that prophets e'er of Bliss foretold,
And all that poets ever feigned of old,
As yielding joy to man, shall now be seen
And ever flourish like an evergreen.
Then mortals join to hail great nature's plan,
That fully gives to Babes those rights it gives to man.

He advertised his schemes also by his broadsides,
placards and handbills. As a rule the broadsides

contained selections from his songs or extracts from his tracts.

Two of these were adorned with coloured drawings signed " W. Spence." One is called the " Disappointed Missionary."

A fat missionary addressed some Red Indians :—

" God has enjoined you to be Christians, pay rent and tithes and become a civilized people."

RED INDIANS.
> If rents we once consent to pay
> Taxes on us you will lay
> And then our freedom's passed away.

The other is entitled " The Contrast," and has a similarly arresting picture ; this time of two Red Indians (left) and the Civilized Ass (right). The ass has two pairs of panniers with the legend :—

> Behold the Civilized Ass
> Two pairs of panniers on his back,
> The first with Rents a heavy mass
> With taxes next his bones do crack.

Undeneath the picture are thirty out of the thirty-one verses of the " Rights of Man " in two columns.

The handbills were generally notices of meetings or advertisements of the Plan. A slip announcing his proposed Spensonian Society formed part of the Secret Committee's collection in 1801.[1] His " A New and Infallible Way to Make Peace " and his " A New and Infallible Way to Make Trade " must be specimens of his bills.[2]

[1] Quoted by Place, 27808, p. 195, from the Appendix to the Second Report, 1801. Place points out that the Report does not say whether it is a handbill, address, or placard.
[2] Vide Spence, " Songs."

Spence's persecutions were responsible for the pamphlets " Case of T. Spence . . . 1792 " and the " Important Trial " (1803 and 1807). Through them he sought to make known both his cause and the afflictions he was enduring in its behalf.

In the midst of all his labours he found time to think of his new alphabet. He intended to publish both a dictionary and a Bible. One number of the Bible survives—a proof sheet—but though he and his son began the dictionary, nothing seems to have come of the project.

All these publications may be regarded as incidental. Developments of the Plan itself must now be followed from the more important publications, the tracts.

Three versions of the lecture survive, " The Rights of Man," 1793, " The Meridian Sun of Liberty," 1796, and that published in " Pigs' Meat," iii, p. 120 (1795). The 1793 and 1795 editions are almost identical, but there are developments in the Plan as published in 1796. Spence now says definitely that it is the landlords who make the laws. He tries to make other statements clearer. He had explained before that the rents collected by the parish authorities would be used in part to pay the parish share of the sum voted by Parliament to the Government. In 1796 he says that the Parliament or National Assembly will decide what the national tax shall be, and that it shall be so much in the pound. One object of his suggestions for dealing with poor strangers was to prevent strangers being looked upon " with an envious eye lest they should become burthensome." He adds in this edition

" by their new neighbours where they have come to reside."

An extra paragraph, beginning " O hearken, ye besotted sons of men," shows that he is being driven by his enemies into a more extreme position. He is bringing his guns to bear upon the upholders of the present system as well as upon the system itself.[1]

Spence, according to the 1793 edition, had anticipated that rents would be lower if his Plan were carried out, as they would no longer be used for a few " haughty, unthankful landlòrds," and there would be other savings effected. He omits this paragraph to make additions to the Plan. He considers more in detail what the parish will do with its lands. Houses, lands or tenements are to be let publicly to the best bidder on a seven years' lease. This will prevent " collusion to the prejudice of the parish revenue and likewise prevent partiality."

" Methinks," he joyfully exclaims, " I now behold the Parish Republics like fraternal or benefit societies, each meet at quarter day to pay their rents and to settle their accounts. . . ."[2] He arranges that his parishes shall have a fixed day for settling up accounts, which shall first have been properly examined. In addition to the sums allocated for government and local expenses, a reserve fund is to be set apart.

A new and delightful idea had occurred to him. There may be a surplus. (He here ignores and later scouts the less delightful one of a deficit.) Disdaining

[1] The bitterness of tone is obvious in most of his publications of 1795-97.
[2] " Meridian Sun," pp. 11-12.

unnecessary details in the way of figures, he estimates that after all public demands are satisfied, there will be a surplus of one-third the total sum received. This is to be divided equally among the parishioners without respect of persons.[1]

> So if by sickness or mischance
> To poverty some wane,
> Their dividends of rents will come
> To set them up again.

" Though I have only spoken of parishioners receiving dividends, which may be understood as if men only were to have the residue of the rents, yet I would have no objection, if the people thought proper, to divide it among the whole number of souls, male and female, married and single, in a parish, from the infant of a day old, to the second infantage of hoary hairs. For as all of every age, legitimate or illegitimate, have a right to live on the public common, and as that common for the sake of cultivation must be let out to rent, that rent then ought to be equally enjoyed by every human being instead of the soil which they are thus deprived of." [2]

This essay shows that Spence was thinking more exactly where his Plan would lead. On the one hand, he pictures the economic life of the community regulated by a federated group of benefit societies whose directors were to be elected from and by the share-

---

[1] Vide " Pigs' Meat," i, p. 42 (1793). " Jubilee Hymn," revised version,

> " Welcome that day draws near,
> For then our rents we share. . . ."

And also " Pigs' Meat," i, p. 261.

[2] " Meridian Sun," final paragraphs, pp. 11, 12.

holders, and on the other, he pictures the same directors and shareholders acting in a political capacity. The interdependence of director and stockholder, the dual rôle each played as politician and economist, would prevent trickery, corruption and undue self-interest, would foster a sense of civic responsibility and develop public spirit.

Two of his most interesting articles were published in his periodicals. These were his accounts of " Spensonia," which appeared in " Pigs' Meat," ii, 1794, and in the " Giant-Killer," 1814. They are both revised versions of " Crusonia." The earlier version is in two parts : " The Marine Republic " and " A Further Account of Spensonia." He imagines emigrants from a country appropriating an island near America and there establishing the Spencean system. They begin with one piece of land approximately the size of a parish, and then, as the population grows, map out fresh land into parishes which they rule in the same manner. Spence himself visits the island. He describes what he sees and narrates the conversation that he had with a Spensonian.

The Spensonian explains why he considers private ownership of landed property to be bad. He is not frightened that it will creep in again, because the institution of the ballot is a safeguard against bribery. The system could not be overthrown by force, because the Spensonians were all soldiers.

The Spensonian conducts the author to a military review. The children were taught manœuvres as part of their school training, the citizens studied the art of war in their spare time. Medals were awarded for proficiency. Each parish and ward held its exercises when convenient to it, but two or three times a year the inhabitants of several parishes met to go through their military exercises " under the eye of a general provided by the state." [1]

" The parishes in different liveries came marching in from every direction with artillery, banners and music. Those who had good hor.es were horsemen and formed into troops according to the colour of their horses " (!).[2] Promotion was gained by merit.

Spence noted that the country was like paradise. There were many gardens, the meadows and pastures were strewn with fruit-trees, and corn was cultivated in rows like garden herbs. " The houses and every-thing about them are so aimably neat and so indicative of domestic happiness . . . that they seem the habita-tion of rational beings worthy the approbation of the Deity. . . ." [3]

These benefits are the result of universal suffrage and the Spensonian system of local government. Each man, through his possession of a vote and through his direct interest in the proper management of the parochial territory, has a feeling of respon-sibility. He can see for himself that his interests are furthered by his exertions. The state needs no mend-ing, so by ceasing to debate over state affairs and by caring for municipal concerns the Spensonian becomes an actor instead of a spectator.

A man may repine because he cannot look upon the land he rents as his own, but individual desires must not be suffered if they are detrimental to a

[1] " Pigs' Meat," ii, p. 212.   [2] Ibid.   [3] Ibid., ii, p. 214.

whole people. If property that had been improved remained in the improvers' hands it would tend to become hereditary. The public should benefit from these improvements. After all, the improver's children are part of the public. " And do you think that the people while a man lives and pays his rent will be so ungenerous as to turn him out of house and farm ? " [1] People should be encouraged to make improvements by offers of medals and premiums ; inventions should be bought at a fair price from the inventor for public use. In Spensonia, Parliament has to purchase and publish the secret, because it is obliged to spend money on what is of public utility.

The version of Spensonia published in the " Giant-Killer " has some important variations. They are to be noticed chiefly in Spence's attention to trade, education, wealth of parishes, stimulus of public zeal and enterprise, and difficulties with foreign foes.

Spence ignores commerce in discussing his Plan, or rather he contents himself with saying that trade must be free and with commenting on the flourishing trade of Spensonia. Evidently he had realized that this was inadequate, that it was not sufficient simply to remark on the internal trade of Spensonia as conducted at the periodic fairs held in each of the parishes. In this version the visitor to Spensonia marvels that there is no foreign commerce. From the reply it can be gathered that free trade has been established, but that the Spensonians are too satisfied with their abundant home trade to go " scrambling and fighting " after foreign trade. His physiocratic attitude can be

[1] " Pigs' Meat," ii, p. 217.

shown from remarks in other publications.[1] " Tillage is a trade that never fails."

According to his " Crusonia " and to his " Interesting Conversation," published with his lecture in 1793, the Spensonians would be an educated people. The parish authorities were to maintain preachers, and to establish schools and public libraries. Candidates for Government offices were to be properly examined to see if they were suitable for the position. In this second version of Spensonia he says that education has prevented Spensonians from being thieves. They have been *taught* that if they pay rents to private individuals they will have no money left to buy extras for themselves. Here Spence is expounding the current notion that a man can be made perfect if he is rightly educated and if his education begins early enough.

Spence realizes that some parishes will be wealthier than others. He instances those which possess mines and fisheries. The legislature must prevent these parishes from being selfish or from being jealous of strangers or foreigners. The Government will also have to arrange that the poorer parishes shall not be over-burdened. Their surplus poor must be sent to wealthier parishes.

Stimulus of public zeal and enterprise will be provided by the emulation of men in elegance and cleanliness, in the arts and in public works, in their gardens, houses and fruit-tree hedges, in trade.

He suggests that there would be no danger from foreign enemies, because the soldiers of the hostile

[1] See in his " Songs," " An Infallible Way to Make Trade," his " Dream," and " Queries."

army could be bought up by paying them double for life! The new army would come and settle in Spensonia and be its most stalwart defence. Their extra money would enable them to spend more and so make trade. There would be no danger from this army, because it could not revolt without the aid of the Spensonians, who would be too satisfied with their Government to assist.

The ludicrous nature of this proposal needs no comment.

After his imprisonment in 1794, Spence published various tracts, the "End of Oppression" in four parts,[1] a "Letter to Ralph Hodge" dealing with grievances of the day—informers, food scarcity, deserted villages—and a third volume of "Pigs' Meat," with its reprint of the lecture. These served to pick up the threads of his work, to answer objections, and to restate his Plan.

He now considers what immediate steps must be taken to put his Plan into action. The country must first be willing to adopt it. It will then require "a few thousands of hearty, determined fellows, well armed and appointed with officers, and having a committee of honest, firm and intelligent men to direct their actions to the proper object." The committee will issue proclamations directing the people in each parish to take possession of the landed property and to appoint a committee to look after it. Each landholder will have to deliver all writings and docu-

[1] "End of Oppression," in two parts, 1795. "Recantation of the End of Oppression," 1795. "A Fragment of Ancient Prophecy," 1796.

ments relating to his estate to the committee that they may be immediately burnt. The last payments due from the tenants would create a fund for immediate use. If the " aristocrats arose to contend the matter, let the people be firm and desperate, destroying them root and branch." The confiscated goods of the aristocrats would pay for the expense of war.[1]

" The Reign of Felicity," 1796, is one of Spence's best dialogues on his Plan, but the announcement on the reverse of the title-page is all that must be considered of its actual matter.

" The annual landed rental of a certain country is said to be Fifty Millions and the Taxes Twenty Millions. And it is also said that the Government of the same country has been and may be administered at the small expense of One Million and a Half. Wherefore, according to the system of the End of Oppression there remains a goodly surplus of Sixty-Eight Millions [2] and a Half of Public Property to be divided among the inhabitants to promote industry, annihilate Misery, and establish a Reign of Felicity."

Spence is realizing that actual figures must be taken into account if his scheme is to be of practical value. This financial effort was not a happy one, but it shows that Spence was thinking along the right lines. Unfortunately, his illustration of the financial working

[1] " End of Oppression." From what he says elsewhere Spence only contemplates civil war as a last resort. Vide " Trial," p. 29, and note where he says he is appealing to the force of reason and is not sounding a tocsin to massacre. In his " Restorer " he says that he realizes the change would be accompanied by an economic upheaval.

[2] Not sixty-eight millions. He has added the taxes and rental together.

of the scheme in " How to Study Politics " [1] was as fallacious as the foregoing announcement.

In his " Rights of Infants," 1797, he gives special consideration to the position of women and children according to the Plan, while two other publications bear testimony to his care that it should be as complete and precise as possible. These are his " Perfect Commonwealth," 1798, and the extended version of it, " The Constitution of Spensonia." Spence was following French fashions in thus drawing up constitutions.

Some mention must be made here of the conversations, queries and catechisms that he prefixed and appended to his publications.

He left no stone unturned to answer to the best of his ability such objections as were raised to his scheme.

He explained his principles in his lectures, he sketched an ideal form of society in his " Spensonia," he grappled as best he could with the financial aspect of the matter, he worked out what he considered a suitable constitution.[2] To his dying day he was labouring to improve his Plan and to make the most of such suggestions as had been offered to him.

His " fame " as a writer must rest on his prose writings rather than on his verse. He is vigorous, direct, and not without humour. His ambiguities arise from his confusion of thought, not from his inability to express himself. He can be violent in his language, but he is never offensive.

[1] Vide the Introduction to his " Perfect Commonwealth."
[2] Vide " Perfect Commonwealth," 1798, and " Constitution of Spensonia," 1803. See Bibliography, Appendix, p. 207–23, for a complete list of his publications.

" I hope," he says in the Preface to the " Rights of Man," the Reader need not be told that I do not in the least intend my own country. . . . I beg to be understood as laying down a system of government for the freeborn unshackled minds of the North American and African Savages who have not yet learned to look upon bloodsucking landlords and state leeches with that timourous superstitious and cringing reverence paid to such miscreants in a country so well bred as this." [1]

" O worse than Molochs," cries the mother of children to the haughty aristocrat, " now let the blood of millions of innocent babes who have perished through your vile usurpations be upon your murderous heads." " Moreover, when we begin with you, we will make a full end of your power at once. We will not unpolitically tamper with the lion and pluck out a tooth now and then." [2]

No wonder his advertisements attracted attention.

ADVERTISEMENT.

THE POISONOUS QUALITIES OF THE PUBLICATION
ENTITLED

" PIGS' MEAT."

A WORK IN THREE VOLUMES.

Price, bound, 6d. each.

The Compiler has evidently selected from the following authors and Works only such passages as unequivocally inculcate and justify modern Politics and Democratic principles. His care in choosing those paragraphs only which contain the most Pith and Argument and in rejecting those of a light, flimsy and temporary nature discover his Vanity

---

[1] Preface to Lecture, 1793, pp. iii, iv.
[2] " Rights of Infants," pp. 3, 7 and 9.

in supposing his Work might be the political instructor of other generations than the present. But how will he be disappointed if the Study of the Rights of Man should become unpopular ? . . . The authors and works, Swift, Cato, etc., follow.[1]

His " Reign of Felicity "—he had a happy knack of choosing attractive titles—is one of the most interesting of his dialogues both for the matter and the liveliness with which it is set forth, and for the shrewdness and ingenuity of the author.

The dialogue[2] takes place in a coffee house between a Courtier, an Esquire, a Clergyman, and a Farmer. The clergyman and the courtier hope that Washington will sow seeds of religion among the Indians, as religion will make them good and submissive.

THE ESQUIRE. It is the way to make blind and slavish subjects, willing preys of Kings and Priests—Church and State have been united from the beginning. I will be sorry if the independent minds of the Indians, " the only freemen remaining on the face of the earth," are poisoned and depraved.

FARMER. I would not like to see the Indians beasts of burden to the Esquire and the Landlords, who have pricely revenues from their rents, and, as they are the most powerful, control the Government. I can show how the Indians could remain free without lords.

COURTIER. Aerial plans may be formed, but the good old way of invasion practised by Israelites, Romans, Goths, Vandals, Saxons, Danes, Normans, Spanish, English, and all other civilizers of mankind is the only way to succeed. They should enter a territory by force, establish themselves in manors, and make the conquered vassals and slaves.

ESQUIRE. " An uncivil way of civilizing the world ! " Our neighbours may take it into their heads to civilize us again the same way. I would suggest a milder way for the

---

[1] Advertisement on the back of the " Recantation of the End of Oppression."

[2] The following is a summary of a portion of the dialogue.

Americans. Landlords are essential to civilization. Everyone has an independent and equal right to the soil, therefore let the Americans cast lots to decide who shall be landlords. The natives and foreigners could rent land from them. Foreigners would introduce arts and sciences.

FARMER. I object to this landlord system. I know a system that would include its advantages. The Indians should pay rents. The question is to whom ? (He then outlines the Spencean system.)

ESQUIRE. I am surprised that civilized Indians shall pay rents.

FARMER. But every species of property must be paid for.

ESQUIRE. I propose equal shares of property, and suggest that land shall be leased to foreigners.

FARMER. I object to this as it is impracticable. (His reasons follow.) No account need be taken of movable property. "It is not worth regarding the trifling influence of movable property alone in the liberties of the people. When wealth cannot be rooted and fixed in land it is of a fluctuating and evaporating nature, and is apt, like the moisture of the earth, to take wings and fly away, unless restored by the flower of industry."

"The good effects of such a change" as his Plan, he says in the "End of Oppression," "would be more exhilarating and reviving to the hunger-bitten and despairing children of oppression than a benign and sudden spring to the frost-bitten earth after a long and severe winter." [1]

[1] "End of Oppression" (2nd edition), p. 9.

CHAPTER IV

REBUFFS AND DISAPPOINTMENTS

SPENCE was the type of man to court trouble. He was willing to take any risk for the sake of his Plan. By selling Paine's pamphlets he was rendering himself liable to prosecution for publishing and selling seditious matter. Members of the Loyal Association [1] were most anxious to bring " traitors " to justice. Spence tells the story of his troubles in this connection in his pamphlet " The Case of Thomas Spence, Book-seller, the Corner of Chancery Lane, London, who was committed to Clerkenwell Prison on Monday, the tenth of December, 1792, for selling the Second Part of Paine's ' Rights of Man.' "

This is Spence's tale :—

" Immediately on the institution of a celebrated Society [2] for preserving places and pensions, Mr. Spence being a poor man and less likely to oppose the lordly menaces of violent Aristocracy was repeatedly surrounded, insulted, and even threatened with his life and the destruction of his little all, if he did not give up part of his bread and decline selling the ' Rights of Man ' and other political tracts. The eagerness

[1] See p. 56–7 for the Loyal Association.
[2] I.e. the " Loyal Association."

of the public mind for political investigation almost rendered it useless for him to keep any other articles, and therefore to a poor man it was indeed a very serious sacrifice unless they had *threatened* him likewise with ample compensation." Even a " pious rector " tried to persuade the landlord to drive him from his stall. " O, Depravity, where is thy blush ! " No one opposed him for selling Burke's writings.[1]

On the morning of Thursday, December 6, 1792, two Bow Street runners came at the instance of Mr. Reeves, the chairman, and bought from Spence *his* " Rights of Man " instead of Paine's. He was arrested and taken to Hatton Gardens. " To the honour of the magistrate " he declined to commit him. Spence told the magistrate that he might as well be committed for selling " Gulliver's Travels," More's " Utopia," Locke on " Government," or Puffendorf on the " Law of Nations." In a note it is stated that the runner called on Mr. Spence and said that he was heartily sick of the whole business—he had never been paid for the book he bought as an information [!]. Spence received no compensation for this injury.

Then, on the following Monday morning, two runners came, bought Paine's " Rights of Man," arrested Spence, and hustled him into a hackney coach. He remonstrated with the " prostituted ruffians " and asked whether he lived in Spain, Turkey, Algiers, or England.[2] He was taken to a public-house in Bow Street. There he had to wait three hours until the magistrate had had his dinner. He was roughly handled—one man took him by the throat—and his

[1] " Case of T. Spence," pp. 4-5.   [2] Ibid., p. 6.

personal possessions, including a book of extracts
from Locke and other writers, were taken from him.
" Perhaps since the days of bloody Queen Mary have
no prisoners under the same circumstances been
treated in so violent a manner as Mr. Spence during
his stay in the public-house." [1]

Spence felt that the proceedings were unjust, as the
pamphlet in question had not been legally proscribed,[2]
but the magistrate justified his action by reference to
the Royal Proclamations and to the opinion of the
Grand Jury. Spence was questioned before the Grand
Jury, a proceeding that he considered wrong, and was
committed to prison. He was again roughly handled
by the runners, who tried to bluff him into hiring a
coach. They threatened to make him walk in chains
through the streets. Spence said that he would wear
the chains. He was taken, without them, to gaol at
11 p.m. He was threatened and ill-treated. He had
to pay one shilling to the turnkey for a bed and one
penny for a candle. The pennyworth of candle meant
a brief look round his cell before he was locked up
and left to undress in the dark. His bed was damp.
The next day he had to herd with felons and to satisfy
their pecuniary demands. Altogether he spent £1 4s.
during the thirty hours that he was in prison before
being bailed out.

Spence published a copy of his commitment " in
order to convince the public that he has been guilty

[1] " Case of T. Spence," p. 6.
[2] Paine's trial did not take place until December 18, 1792, but
his publisher Jordan had been summoned in the May previous,
and Paine himself only escaped arrest by twenty minutes in the
September when he fled the country.

of no other crime than what is alleged here against him."

Middlesex to wit.   To the keeper of the New Prison at Clerkenwell.   Receive into your custody the body of Thomas Spence, herewith sent you, brought before me, Sir Sampson Wright, Knt., one of His Majesty's Justices of the Peace in and for the said county, by Robert Berresford, Constable, and charged before me the said Justice, upon the oath of John De la Fontaine and the said Robert Berresford, for publishing and selling at Chancery Lane in the said County of Middlesex, a certain seditious book or pamphlet called, " Rights of Man, part the second, containing Principle and Practice by Thomas Paine," tending to inflame the minds of His Majesty's subjects, and create disturbances against the peace, etc.   Him, therefore, safely keep in your said custody for want of sureties or until he shall be discharged by due course of law, and for so doing this shall be your sufficient warrant.

Given under my hand and seal this tenth day of December 1792.

SAMPSON WRIGHT.

(*True Copy*.)

THOMAS ROBERTS, *Clerk*.
SAMUEL NEWPORT, *Keeper*.[1]

Spence gives us no further information about this trial except that the jury found a True Bill and that he was awaiting a judicial decision.   Hone says : " I know that Spence was arrested when he kept the long Stall in Chancery Lane at the Middle Row corner, for I was passing at the time and I heard him in dispute with the officer.   He had just got his shutters down in the morning when he was pounced upon.   It was early, therefore, and no one but myself was present at first.   I only remained a minute or so,

[1] " Case of T. Spence," p. 16.

for I had to hasten to a situation I then had to attend at 9 o'clock. . . ." [1]

In two letters,[2] one published in the *Morning Post* of December 18, 1794, and the other published in the *Morning Chronicle*, January 3, 1795, Spence describes his troubles 1792–94.

SIR,
    My second volume of " Pigs' Meat " was finished on that memorable day, the seventeenth of May, 1794, the day on which the Commons passed the Suspension of the Habeas Corpus Act and terror being the order of the day, you declined inserting my advertisement. On the Tuesday following, May 20th, I was dragged to the Secretary of the State's Office under pretence of being charged with treasonable practices, and from thence in a few days committed to Newgate where I yet, to the honour of the Government, remain untried. But finding that on account of my long imprisonment the business of my shop is much decayed, I have essayed once more to get my book advertised. . . .

I am, Sir, etc.,
T. SPENCE.

NEWGATE, HIGH TREASON SIDE.
    December 17th, 1794.

FELLOW-CITIZENS,
    I am again restored to my shop, after a tedious confinement of more than seven months, but change of circumstances renders my return productive of but small joy. But though the *public enemy* has acquired the satisfaction of reducing me to the inability of carrying on my little business with my wonted alacrity, yet I trust I shall not be quite overlooked by the patrons of the *Martyrs of Freedom* [3] in the dispensation of their favours. I beg leave therefore to observe to the friends of freedom and political truth that by assisting me in the sale of my book called

Pigs' Meat

---

[1] Hone to Place, 27808, p. 314.
[2] Spence, " Pigs' Meat," iii, pp. 3–4.
[3] Hardy, Horne Tooke, Thelwall, etc., leaders of the Corresponding Society.

they will not only essentially serve me, but will also contribute greatly to the enlightening of mankind. Since the prosecution began in 1792, I have been four times dragged from my business by runners and messengers. Three times have I been indicted before grand Juries, and twice have they found true bills. Thrice have I been lodged in prison for different periods of time and once have I been put to the *bar*, but never once convicted.[1] Neither did my son (a boy of twelve years of age) escape a prison for selling in the streets the *Rights of Man* in verse (price only one halfpenny), the poems which he had were confiscated and I paid a *fine*. Thus the mighty affair ended. And for what has all this been ? Why, for doing those things which my own rights and the rights of mankind would not suffer me to dispense with and which to decline would have been to betray the liberties of my country.

I am, etc.,
T. SPENCE.

No 8, LITTLE TURNSTILE, HIGH HOLBORN.
Dec. 22*nd*, 1794.

Three newspaper cuttings[2] in Place's collection supplement Spence's letters.

January 16th, 1793.—Thomas Spence who kept a bookstall at the Corner of Chancery Lane and was some time ago taken into custody for selling the Second Part of Paine's " Rights of Man," was again apprehended on Sunday, by one of the Bow Street officers, by virtue of a Bench Warrant (a bill of indictment having been found against him by the Grand Jury for Middlesex) and carried before Sir Sampson Wright, and committed to the New Prison, Clerkenwell, where he will remain until he give bail for his appearance at the next Quarter-Sessions.

After his release in December,[3] Spence seems to have been re-arrested, although apparently he had

---

[1] Is Spence adopting the rôle of St. Paul ?
[2] Place, Add. MSS., 27808, pp. 254-5. The date has been written upon each cutting, i.e. January 16, 1793, February 1793, December 6, 1793.
[3] Place, Add. MSS., 27808, p. 199.

found bail.   Perhaps he had not fulfilled the conditions in relation to his bail.

The second cutting, February 1793, says that the Solicitor-General attended at Hicks' Hall to prosecute several persons " indicted at the suit of the Crown for selling and speaking libels against His Majesty and the present Government." Spence, the Poor Pamphleteer, was first put to the Bar and indicted for selling the Second Part of Paine's " Rights of Man." Spence was acquitted, because the pages in the information assigned as libellous were at variance with those on record.

The third cutting, December 1793, says :—

On Friday last three indictments were preferred against Mr. Spence, Bookseller in Little Turnstile, Holborn, by the Attorney-General for selling Paine's [? Spence's] " Rights of Man in Verse," and another weekly publication under the title of " Pigs' Meat." After due examination the three were thrown out.

With the aid of the newspaper cuttings, Spence's letter to the *Morning Chronicle* may be checked and his troubles with the authorities in London, 1792–94, summarized. In December 1792 he was arrested and a True Bill was found. In January 1793 he was again arrested, apparently in connection with the True Bill of December, and, having been put to the Bar, he was tried in February 1793. Presumably he was acquitted, as there is no further mention of the matter. In the following December (1793) a True Bill having been found, three indictments were preferred against him, but were thrown out. Thus he was twice acquitted, three times indicted, once put to the Bar.

In May 1794 he was arrested and kept in prison seven months without a trial. This accounts for the four arrests and the three sojourns in prison.

His first prosecutions were for selling Paine's literature, the remainder were due to the sale of his own.

He was harassed by minor troubles, too ; when he returned to his stall after his first arrest, he found three papers on the shutters saying " that the owner was in gaol for selling seditious books and that they [?] hoped it would be a warning to the others." [1]

On Thursday, December 13, 1792, when Parliament opened, a gentleman, " or one who aimed to be thought so," seized the First Part of Paine's " Rights of Man " [2] from a young man who was reading it at Spence's stall, " and in a curious (alias Grub Street) dialect abused Mr. Spence, hustled him about, tore his short, and dragged him to an adjoining shop, where joined by more of his *brutal fraternity*, he robbed the poor man of two other books." One hastened to fetch the runners, while the others secured Spence. Luckily for him the spectators interfered.[3]

On Christmas Eve his landlord's daughter brought him a written notice to quit his stall by Lady Day, 1793. Her father's customers, among them the " pious rector," were complaining, and he did not wish to offend them.[4]

Spence's son was arrested for selling his publications, and later one of the small boys employed by him for

[1] ' Case of T. Spence," 1792, p. 9.
[2] Ibid. It was only the Second Part that had been " proscribed."
[3] Ibid., p. 10.   [4] Ibid., p. 11.

the same purpose was also arrested. This boy and his mother lodged with Spence.[1]

Even his selling of saloup was a source of difficulties. A rival saloup keeper at the opposite corner had secured for himself the protection of the street-keepers and constables. Through them he contrived to have Spence summoned as a nuisance. The arguments of the pair convinced the magistrate that the rival was equally a nuisance and that Spence had been summoned for private interest. The case was dismissed.[2]

Spence was bitterly disappointed at the result of his efforts. His Plan was not acclaimed as he had hoped, nor did he win any recognition from fellow-reformers. He had occupied the time that he spent in " black Newgate " in writing verses. He had prophesied the downfall of " feudal tyranny," and had fortified himself with the reflection that though he was often in prison he still kept to his song " the rights of man for me." He wrote to the papers to remind the " Martyrs of Freedom," the political reformers imprisoned by the Government in 1794, that he was of their number, and to his chagrin he was completely overlooked. Place says that the verses in " Pigs' Meat " " On the Late Barren Patriotic Meetings " had their source in his disappointment. The " patriots " had celebrated their release by dinners.

---

[1] " Pigs' Meat," iii, p. 4; H.O. papers, 119.
[2] Mitchell tells this story in the *Newcastle Magazine*, January 1821. The pair must have been of the " race of industrious imitators " of Mr. Read, the owner of the only *Salopian House* in Fleet Street, the south side. The chimney sweep and artisan could have a " sumptious basin " of this fragrant beverage for 1½d., and a slice of bread and butter ½d. Lamb, " The Praise of Chimney Sweepers."

Spence considered that their money might have been more worthily spent.

On the late Patriotic Meetings, particularly that on the 4th of February, 1795.

> The People's friends, see how they meet
> All in the dumps with nought to eat
> And prudently give up reform
> To bend their force against the storm.
> But nought afford to give relief
> To patr'ot woe or patr'ot grief.

The Foxites and Stanhopites each meet.

> But nought afford to give relief
> To patr'ot woe or patr'ot grief.
>
> .   .   .   .   .
>
> If half the wealth and half the wind
> That there was spent to no great end
> Had been employed for to relieve
> The wants of patr'ots that now grieve
> It would have caused without alloy
> For years to come equisite joy.
>
> But sighs now follow prison groans
> And duns and landlords in their turns
> The place of gaolers stern supply.
>
> .   .   .   .   .
>
> Farewell ye gorging parties then
> Go feed like swine, ye are not men
> What e'er your parties you may call
> You're all alike so d'mn you all.[1]

T. S.

February 8th, 1795.

Spence was too proud to ask the " patriots " for help. In his " Recantation of the End of Oppression," 1796, and " Rights of Infants," 1797, he deplores his

[1] " Pigs' Meat," iii, p. 56.

failure to enlist the sympathy even of those whose worldly lot he was anxious to improve.

He was not, however, entirely friendless, nor did he fail to find some sympathy.   When he was attacked at his stall the spectators had interfered and had rescued him from " the hands of the most *diabolical* and lawless banditti that ever threatened the peace of the Metropolis."   At the end of the pamphlet there is a short paragraph.

A subscription being opened for the Defence of the poor Man whose Case is described in the Pamphlet, any persons wishing to contribute for the purpose, will please to pay their subscriptions to Mr. Hamilton, Bookseller, near Gray's Inn, Holborn, where a book for the purpose lays open.[1]

It is to this period of his life that the story of his second marriage belongs.   Mackenzie says that his first wife died in the north, and that soon after her death Spence chanced to see a pretty girl cleaning some steps.   He went up to her and asked her if she would like to be married.   She consented to marry him because she wanted to punish her first lover. As might be expected, she soon deserted him.   She fled to the West Indies with a sea-captain.   A letter preserved by Place says that she deserted him at the time of his first [?] imprisonment in 1794.[2]   When she came back to England, she returned to her husband, who forgave her.   " But the safety of his health and property at length compelled him to dismiss her from the house."[3]   His partner " turned

[1] " Case of T. Spence," pp. 9–16.
[2] Place, 27808, p. 229.   The writer probably meant his first *long* imprisonment.
[3] Mackenzie, " Memoir."

out to be a star whose malefic influence not only marred his peace of mind, and defeated many of his good intentions, but obstructed in some degree the progress of his plans for the general improvement of the condition of mankind. So much was she the termagant that he often compared himself to Socrates, who was cursed during his life with the scolding Xanthippe." [1] Spence allowed her 8s. a week as long as he lived. In the fourth letter of his " Restorer " he advocates greater facilities for divorce. He thinks that men might be more willing to give erring women another chance if they could divorce them more easily. These opinions may have had their origin from his own domestic troubles. He thought that it was terrible for anyone to be tied permanently to a spendthrift, a drunkard, a sluggard, a tyrant, a brute, a trollop, or a vixen. His treatment of his wife won him the admiration of his friends.[2]

It was after giving up the Chancery Lane Stall that Spence settled at No. 8, Little Turnstile, High Holborn. This shop, which he christened the " Hive of Liberty," was in a narrow lane. Two open spaces just under the shop and in a line with its cellars occupied the whole of the foot pavement. They were let to people who sold greengroceries and old clothes.[3] This was his home until the end of 1796, or the beginning of 1797. Here he entered on a more lucrative business than letting lodgings or selling pamphlets. He became a token-dealer, though his pen was as active as ever. His new occupation

[1] Davenport, p. 2.
[2] Place, Add. MSS., 27808, pp. 227-9.   [3] Ibid., p. 182.

afforded him an excellent opportunity of advertising his scheme.

The copper currency of the country,[1] especially towards the end of the eighteenth century, was in such a neglected condition, the supply was so meagre and the design so inferior that tons of imitation regal halfpennies and farthings were in circulation. The Parys Copper Mines Company in Anglesey issued halfpennies and pennies of its own, stamped with its own device. They were preferred by the miners because of their superior value. Other companies and trades followed suit, partly for advertisement, partly for convenience. These tokens were stamped with some device appropriate as ornament or advertisement, or significant of some current event. It became the fashion to collect the token coins. The mania so grew that token-dealing developed into quite a business, and the ranks of the genuine collectors were swelled by the hosts of those who merely collected tokens as a passing whim. Consequently dealers began to manufacture " sets " of tokens. Skidmore, a London dealer, issued a series stamped with representations of London churches. The " true " collectors were much annoyed by the spurious tokens and the frauds that unscrupulous dealers practised. The copper was

[1] This account is from A. Waters, " Trial of Thomas Spence," 1917, from Dalton and Hamer's " Provincial Token Coinage of the Eighteenth Century," 1910, and from the *Gentleman's Magazine*, 1796-98. The correspondence of " R. Y." and " Civis " in the magazine, 1796-97, led " C. H.," Gray's Inn, to write four essays on the subject which were published in the magazine for 1798. According to Waters, " C. Sh." is " C. Shepherd." According to ' C. Sh.'s " note, *Gentleman's Magazine*, January–June 1798, p. 12, " Civis " is a Mr. Wright, a well-known collector. " R. Y." has not been traced.

" bad." Scarce coins were counterfeited. Dies were used as obverses and reverses to different coins. Twenty-eight coins could be manufactured from seven dies. Hence confusion reigned. " Skidmore of Holborn was one of the most reprehensible dealers," but he was partly forgiven because of the beauty of his coins.

The fashion was at its height in 1794, but the trade declined when the Government, alarmed by the increasing number of counterfeit coins, stopped the issue of tokens.

Spence not only dealt in genuine tokens, but also in tokens of his own manufacture. Place says that he had blank pieces of metal cut out which he struck with a punch.[1] Mackenzie describes how he jerked the coins from his window among the passers-by in order to advertise his scheme.[2] He was a well-known dealer, and his coins were regarded as curios. " C. Sh."[3] suggesting that collections of tokens may be historically useful, says: " on Spence's coins may be traced the republican politics of the enemies of the present Government."[4] He also did good service to collectors. The confusion caused by the dealers and the number of coins in existence complicated the task of collectors. Early in 1795 Spence issued a catalogue, " which immediately eclipsed " that issued by Hammond in the previous year, " as it was arranged in

---

[1] Place, 27808, p. 182. 　　　　[2] Mackenzie, " Memoirs."
[3] The four essays were published as follows: *Gentleman's Magazine*, January–June 1798 : I. January, p. 10 ; II. February, p. 118 ; III. March, p. 212 ; July–December 1798 : IV. September, p. 179.
[4] Essay I, p. 13.

alphabetical order." " An appendix chiefly containing
the names of Spence's own coins appeared soon afterwards." [1]   In spite of the obvious sincerity that this
action displays, the genuine collectors were most
wrathful with Spence.   Skidmore, " C. Sh." considers,
" does not deserve so much censure as Spence, the
author of some contemptible political pamphlets.
This man could impugn the character of the administration and plead as an advocate for public justice
and yet had not private honesty to recommend *himself*.
His dies were numerous and they were interchanged
almost beyond the powers of human calculation.
The designs of many of his pieces were contemptible
and illiberal in the extreme . . . they were struck in a
very careless and awkward manner upon the most
corrupt of copper." [2]   " The vanity of the publisher
is only equalled by his contemptible artifice and his
personal head is scarcely more valuable than the coin
that bears its resemblance." [3]

" Civis " thinks that " R. Y." is peevish on the
subject of bad coins.[4]   The trifling " political jettons
of Spence and others " are only rude caricature, and
the less attention is paid to them the better.   " R. Y.",
who had not actually referred to Spence by name,
replies to " Civis."   " It is not long since I called at

[1] Essay II, p. 118.   [2] Ibid., p. 121.
[3] *Gentleman's Magazine*, 1798, Essay III, p. 212.
[4] The correspondence essential to the present purpose is as
follows :—
Gentleman's Magazine, 1796 : September, " R. Y." wrote a
letter on the subject of tokens ; December, Charles Pye answers.
Gentleman's Magazine, 1797 : January-June, p. 301, " Civis "
complains that " R. Y." is peevish ; pp. 267-70, " R. Y." replies ;
p. 270, another letter from " Civis " ; June, p. 471, letter from
" R. Y."

Spence's shop and saw many thousands of different tokens lying in heaps and selling at what struck me to be great prices." These, therefore, could not [as " Civis " had suggested] " be considered as struck for a limited sale. . . . With ' Civis ' I can value merit in whatever shape it may appear, and it is not because a jetton proceeds from the shop of one of the three Thomases that I would reject it, but because having no merit in the execution, I see no good, but many bad purposes answered by encouraging its circulation." [1] However, " R. Y.'s " anxieties were set at rest. " Spence experienced the punishment of his dishonesty and became a bankrupt." [2]

" R. Y." writes in June 1797 :—

I have been informed that Mr. Spence has quitted the business of dealing in coins and has disposed of his dies principally, if not entirely, to a dealer in Holborn.

It is good to think that Spence should have had even this brief spell of comparative prosperity and renown.

One of his tokens has already been described. A few more have been selected at random from his catalogue.

No. 67.   Cat. A farthing. In Society live like me. R. A hand referring to the Political Bible, " Pigs' Meat." Motto : If Lords all mankind are, they the Rents should share.

418.   Spence (T.) his head. Seven months imprisoned for high treason in 1794. R. Same as Deserted Village.

---

[1] " R. Y.," April 1797. The three Thomases are T. Horne Tooke, T. Hardy (= Martyrs of Freedom), and T. Spence. Their three heads are represented on one of Spence's tokens.
[2] *Gentleman's Magazine*, 1798, Essay II.

419. His head. Farthing size. R. Rouse Britannia.
576. Deserted Village. A village in ruins. One only
      Master grasps the Whole Domain. R. Britannia
      confounded, the cap of liberty falling to the ground.
      Motto : Rouse Britannia.

The cat was a favourite of his, because, like himself,
it would be stroked down, but not against the grain.
One coin has a cat with the motto : " My freedom I
among slaves enjoy." Another favourite had a
" Meridian Sun," with Nov. 8th, 1775, in the centre.
Motto : " Spence's glorious Plan is Parochial Partnership In Land Without Private Property." [1]

One of Spence's advertisements runs as follows :—

New Coins published and sold by T. Spence, Dealer in
Coins, Number 8, Little Turnstile, High Holborn. 1. His
Head. 2. A Pig [etc., etc., 20 in all].

N.B.—The above being under dies may be said to be
obverses, and the following being upper dies may be struck
as reverses to any of them, which has in general been done.
Wherefore when any of the above obverses are wrote for,
let it be mentioned which or whether all of the following
reverses be wanted. Reverses that may be struck with any
of the following obverses, viz. . . . [20 reverses follow]. [2]

No wonder Spence was the despair of the collectors !
His failure as a token-dealer may have been the
cause of his removal to a small shop at No. 9, Oxford
Street. The " Rights of Infants " was published
early in 1797, and it announces that he has lately
removed from No. 8, Little Turnstile. Or perhaps
the death of his son accounts for it. He is as reticent

[1] Vide description of the coin struck for him by Jeremiah,
above, p. 54.
[2] From one of the two copies of the " Coin Collectors' Companion "
in the Goldsmiths' Library. The advertisement follows p. vi. of the
" Companion."

about his boy as he is about all his private affairs. He mentions him in reference to his arrest for selling his father's broadsheets, but that is all. Hone told Place that the son died in his youth, and that the last time he saw him was about 1797, when Spence was preparing a dictionary.[1]

Spence's letter (1800) complaining of the hospitals is surely reminiscent of personal experience. He complains that patients are kept waiting for letters of admission, that out-patients are not promptly attended to by the doctor, and that security for funeral expenses is demanded. People with infectious diseases, he says, should be made to go to hospital, and those who give information of infectious cases should be rewarded. Small-pox would thus be eradicated.[2] The letter gives an idea of some of life's hardships in 1800, and may be connected with his son's death.

[1] Hone to Place. Place, 27808, p. 314.
[2] " Restorer," Letter XIII.

CHAPTER V

THE IMPORTANT TRIAL

SPENCE can never have had many friends. His intolerance, his irritability and his discourtesy, rather than his rags and his poverty, would repel adherents. Francis Place, who appreciated his real worth, was always glad to see him. They never quarrelled, though they rarely agreed, and Spence " often uttered very severe expressions." [1]

Spence probably came to know Place through his connection with the London Corresponding Society. His acquaintance with Thomas Evans, and with the latter's brother-in-law Galloway, must have originated in the same manner.

Place says that Galloway and Evans were two of the cleverest members of the London Corresponding Society, and that Galloway refused to desert the Society when it had fallen on evil days. Bamford describes Galloway as a cool, methodical man of business. When Place first knew him he was a mechanic in Holborn. When Bamford knew him he had both a town house and a country house, which was the resort of scientific and literary men of all classes.

Evans's trade was that of a colourer of prints in

[1] Place, 27808, p. 155.

1798. Afterwards he became a patent brace-maker. Hone describes him as he saw him at work in his little shop, No. 8, Newcastle Street, Strand. " . . . he appeared to me one of the plainest and most honest-minded men I ever saw. . . . He had . . . a round, good, healthy, fat-looking face, the very index of a manly mind, and his speech was as bold and English as his appearance." [1]

Thomas Evans became Secretary of the London Corresponding Society just when the extravagance and violence of some members was making the Government regard it with the utmost suspicion. Their activities began to alarm the Government, especially from 1796. The root of the Government's fear was in the condition of Ireland. Agents of Irish revolutionary societies, notably of the United Irishmen, were intriguing with France and were making catspaws of ignorant republican enthusiasts in England. Thomas Evans, one of these enthusiasts, wanted to establish a republic by means of a revolution. He was promoting a real " revolutionary " society, the United Englishmen, and he was involved in the toils of O'Quigley and his agents, who were engaged in carrying communications between Ireland and France via England.[2]

Place, who knew Evans better than Hone did, thought that he was honest, sincere and talented. " He was a strange creature with very contemptible

---

[1] Hone wrote this in 1816. *Reformists' Register*, October 1817, p. 426.

[2] " Report of the Secret Committee," 1799, the Appendix to the Report, the " Reports of the Secrecy Committee," in the " Parliamentary History and Annual Register " for that year, give the Government's account of its actions.

reasoning powers, a sort of absurd fanatic, continually operated upon by impulses." He was " a fanatic of a peculiar description, ignorant, conceited and remarkably obstinate. Such a man could only have been secretary when the Society had proceeded a long way in its decline." According to Bamford, Evans was wordy and intemperate.[1]

The years 1797–1801 were full of anxiety for the English Government. The rebellion in Ireland, the financial crisis and the mutinies in the fleet, made manifest the wisdom of repressing troublous agitators, especially when it was found that these agitators were encouraging sailors to mutiny and were even trying to rouse a mutinous spirit among the soldiers quartered near the seaports.

The leaders of the London Corresponding Society, Evans and Crosfield, the President, drew up an address to the Irish reminding them of all the cruelties that they had suffered at the hands of the English. After apostrophizing the Irish in general, the address is directed to the English soldiers and then to the nation.

May your governors be warned by historic experience, and learn that Governments are made for the people and not the people for the Governments, that the voice of God is always to be gathered from the congregated will of His rational creatures, that the *just* revenge of a people is ever *proportioned* to the injuries which they have received. . . . In thy behalf, O Ireland, do we supplicate the great Author of Nature !—*January* 30, 1798.[2]

Evans refused to be warned of the danger that he was running, although Place tried his best to deter

[1] Place, 27808, pp. 30, 91, 105. Bamford, ii, p. 112.
[2] " Report of the Committee of Secrecy of the House of Commons," Appendix No. 9, p. 32.

him. He did not realize that O'Quigley was merely using him as a catspaw, though O'Quigley's trial should have rendered him cautious. It came out in the trial that O'Quigley had spent a night at Evans's house. Evans, who is described as a colourer of prints, Plough Court, Fetter Lane, and his wife were cited as witnesses, though they were not called upon to give evidence. In spite of this Evans still tried to form his society of United Englishmen, although the meetings of both the United English and the London Corresponding Society were infested with spies, and Evans himself had been accused of treacherous dealings with the Government.

On April 18, 1798, Evans held a meeting of the United Englishmen to discuss the establishment of a branch society. Several members of the London Corresponding Society attended in order to prevent the continuance of mischief. They were all arrested, and the Government was enabled to keep them in prison without a trial as a Suspension Act had just been past. Evans had a list of Corresponding Society members in his pocket, and the arrest of these followed the next day. Besides this list a copy of the oath to be taken by the True Britons or United Englishmen was also found in Evans's pocket.

I ——— do truly and sincerely engage to defend my country should necessity require, for which purpose I am willing to join the Society of True Britons to learn the use of arms in order that equal rights and laws should be established and defended.[1]

Poor Evans paid dearly for his revolutionary fervour.

[1] "Report of the Committee of Secrecy," Appendix No. II.

In his Introduction to " Christian Policy the Salvation of the Empire," he says :—

I am not an author by profession, but one of those individuals who in the year 1798 incurred so much unjust odium and persecution as reformers, jacobins and levellers. Being at that time Secretary of the London Corresponding Society I was seized on the authority of a general warrant (an arbitrary mandate of the Duke of Portland, an instrument of power declared illegal in the Courts of Law), and after laying [sic] several days on the floor in Tothill Fields Prison was conveyed to the Bastille,[1] and there confined many months in a cell with the accommodation of a bag of straw, a blanket, a rug, denied books, pen, ink, paper, candle, and much of the time access to the fire. Meanwhile my house in the city of London was taken possession of by a corps of Bow Street officers who, after sending my wife and infant son to the Bastille, detained all persons calling thereat (whatever their business) and sent them to prison, finally abandoning the house to chance. At the end of sixteen months' confinement in this Bastille I was banished by authority of an Act of Parliament (passed for that purpose) to the gaol of Winchester, and there imprisoned in a cell twenty-one weeks with the accommodation of a bag of straw, etc., as before ; denied as before books, pen, ink, paper, fire, candle, etc., or society of any sort.* Removed from thence to London I was again banished to the gaol of Chelmsford, and confined under the same regulations and instructions in company with three other persons.

* [Note.] The written instructions to the gaoler from this said Duke of Portland directed him to take from my person any money or other valuables in my possession and to administer the same for any use in such way as he (the gaoler) should think proper. . . . In all two years and eleven months was I immured on the vague and undefined charge of treasonable practices, and then discharged without trial, remuneration or redress. . . . Mr. Pitt and Company had an indemnity bill passed.[2]

---

[1] House of Correction, Middlesex.
[2] Evans is correct. The letters giving these directions about him and his fellow-prisoners are in the Home Office, Entry Books, 119. 2.

Evans's petition to the House was in vain.   Elsewhere [1] he says that his wife was in a delicate state
of health when she was arrested, and that he himself
had suffered ever since from a kind of dropsy in the
legs.   Sometimes he was an invalid for eighteen
months at a stretch.   Though Place did what he
could to help the prisoners, Evans was ruined.

Spence was already in the disfavour of the authorities.
His connection with the London Corresponding Society
and his friendship with Thomas Evans were not calculated to allay their suspicions.   A " Constitution of
the London Corresponding Society " among the papers
collected by the Committee of Secrecy in 1799 states
that it is sold by Thomas Spence of No. 8, Little
Turnstile, Holborn.[2]

Evans says that Spence was arrested in 1798 and
lodged in Cold Bath Fields Prison.   The condition of
the Cold Bath Fields Prison and the conduct of the
Governor Aris were notorious.   Hone reports one of
the " journeymen treason-hunters employed under
Messrs. Portland, Grenville and Company," as having
a vague recollection of Spence and thinking that he
must be a treason-maker.   " D—nme," said he, " I
must have my little ' Pigs' Meat,' and in I popped
on him and lodged him in Aris's hotel."   Spence was
examined two or three times and then released.[3]

The state of Ireland and the conduct of certain

[1] Vide his petition to the House of Commons, 1817.
[2] Vide Appendix to the " Second Report of the Committee of
Secrecy," 1799.
[3] Evans, " Life of Spence," 1821. Hone's " Broadsheets," No. 3,
1816. Place's Journals, 39, 1811–18. A Special Commission was
appointed to inquire into the state of affairs at Cold Bath Fields.
It issued its Report 1801.

disaffected persons in Great Britain led the Government in 1801 to press for a continuation of the Suspension Act. A Select Committee was appointed to inquire into matters.

The first report of April 13th simple states that the seditious practices of 1799 had never been abandoned.

It was at this critical time that Spence chose to publish his pamphlet the " Restorer of Society to its Natural State." The " Restorer " was published on April 10th. On April 19th Spence was arrested in accordance with the information filed against him by the Attorney-General. The extracts from the pamphlet given in the indictment are actual quotations from the " Restorer." The indictment charges Thomas Spence, late of the parish of Saint Anne within the liberty of Westminster, in the county of Middlesex, labourer, " being a malicious, seditious and ill-disposed person, and being greatly disaffected to our said Lord the King and to the Government and constitution of this realm as now by law established. And maliciously and seditiously devising and intending to excite a spirit of discontent and disaffection in the minds of the liege subjects of our said Lord the King . . . and to cause the same subjects to think and believe that the ownership and enjoyment of Land in this country, by the present owners and Proprietors thereof according to law are the causes of evil and oppression to the People of this Realm and as far as in him the said Thomas Spence lay, to move and persuade the same subjects to overturn and destroy the rights of property in Land as now by law established and to take away their land from the present lawful owners and pro-

prietors thereof, within this realm on the tenth day
of April . . . with force and arms, etc. . . ." With
publishing, causing and procuring to be published " a
certain malicious, scandalous and seditious libel containing therein divers scandalous, malicious matters
and things and concerning property in land . . . and
also of and concerning the people and affairs of this
realm (that is to say) * societies,[1] families and tribes
being originally nothing but banditties they esteemed
war and pillage to be honourable and the greatest
ruffians seizing on the principal shares of the soil as
well of land as of movables introduced into the
world all the cursed variety of Lordship, vassalage
and slavery as we see at this day. Now citizens if
we really want to get rid of these evils from amongst
men we * (*meaning the people of this realm*) * must
destroy not only personal and hereditary lordship
but the cause of them which is private property in
land for this is the pillar that supports the temple of
aristocracy.* And in another part thereof according
to the terror and effect following (that is to say)
* then what can be the cure but this ? Namely,
that the Land * (meaning property in land in this
country) shall no longer be suffered to be the property
of individuals but of parishes. The rents of the
parish estates shall be deemed the equal property of
Man, Woman and Child, whether old or young, rich
or poor, legitimate or illegitimate.* And in another
part. . . . * Thus citizen, you see I have put my

---

[1] Spence published the indictment with both editions of his
" Important Trial " (1803 and 1807). Portions between asterisks
(inserted) are to mark the quotations from his pamphlets.

People in a way to destroy all monopoly, and also effectually to provide against even real Famines with ease, and all by the simple operation of rendering the People what they ought to be, Lords of their Own districts.* And in another part. . . . * It is childish, therefore, to expect, ever to see small farms appear again, or ever to see anything else than the utmost screwing and grinding of the Poor, till you quite overturn the present system of Landed Property. . . . For they have got more completely into the spirit and power of oppression now than was ever known before, and they hold the People in defiance by means of their Armed Associations. They are now like a Warlike Enemy quartered upon us for the purpose of raising contributions, and William the Conqueror and his Normans were fools to them in the Arts of Fleecing, therefore anything short of a total destruction of the power of these Samsons will not do, and that must be accomplished, not by simple sharing which leaves the roots of their strength to grow again. No, we must scalp them, or else they will soon recover and pull our temple of liberty about our ears. We must not leave even their stump in the Earth, like Nebuchadnezzar, though guarded by a band of Iron. For ill-destroyed Royalty and Aristocracy will be sure to recover and overspread the earth as before and when they are suffered to return again to their former dominion, it is always with tenfold more rage and policy, and so the condition of their wretched subjects is quickly rendered worse as a reward for their too tender resistance. In plain English, nothing less than the complete extermination of the present system of holding land . . . in the manner I propose will ever bring the world again to a state worth living in. But how is this mighty work to be done ? I answer it must be done at once, for it will be sooner done at once than at twice or a hundred times. For the Public mind being suitably prepared by reading my little tracts and conversing on the subject, a few contiguous parishes have only to declare the Land to be theirs, and form a convention of parochial Delegates ; other adjacent parishes would immediately on being invited follow the example and send also their delegates ; and thus would a Beautiful and Powerful New Republic instantaneously arise in full vigour. The power and resources of war passing in this manner in a moment into the hands of the People from the Hands of the Tyrants, they like shorn Samsons, would become weak and harmless as other men, and being thus, as it were, scalped of their Revenues and the Lands that produced them, their power would never more grow to enable them to overturn our Temple of Liberty. Therefore, talk no more of impossibilities. How lately have we seen unions of the People sufficiently grand and well conducted to give some hopes of success ? Abroad and at home, in America, France, and in our own Fleets we have seen enough of Public Spirit and extensive unanimity in the present generation to accomplish schemes of infinitely greater difficulty than anything that may be done in a day, when once the public mind is duly prepared. In fact it is like the Almighty saying, ' Let there be light and it was so.' So People have only to say. Let the Land be ours and it will be so.

For who, pray, are to hinder the People of any nation from doing so when they are inclined ? Are the Landlords in the parishes more numerous and powerful in proportion to the People than the brave warlike officers in our Mutinous Fleets were to their Crews ? Certainly not. Then Landsmen have nothing to fear more than the seamen, and indeed, much less, for after such a mutiny on land, the Masters of the People would never become their Masters again, whereas the poor sailors had to submit again to their former masters as they well knew to their cost, and as they accomplish their mutinies without bloodshed, so may Landsmen be assured if unanimous, of accomplishing their deliverance in the same harmless manner * . . ."

The second count against Spence for " maliciously . . . devising, contriving, and intending . . . on the tenth day of April in the forty-first year of the reign aforesaid . . . a certain other . . . seditious libel containing therein concerning the rights and property in Land and the People and affairs of this Realm " is based on the same extracts.

" 3rd Count. And the said Attorney-General . . . giveth the court here further to understand . . . that at the time of the Publishing of the malicious and seditious libel . . . there was and yet is open and Public War carried on between our said Lord the King and the persons exercising the powers of government in France and the French . . . the said Thomas Spence . . . contriving and unlawfully, maliciously, seditiously intending and devising to move and excite the liege subjects of our said Lord the King to hatred and dislike of the Government and Constitution of this Realm, as now by Law established and to weaken and destroy in the minds of His Majesty's subjects the disposition to due and vigourous resistance against His Majesty's enemies . . . to the tenor and effect following (that is to say), * What must I say to the French if they come ? If they jeeringly ask me what I am fighting for ? Must I tell them for my country ? For my dear country in which I dare not pluck a nut ? Would they not laugh at me ? Yes, and do you think that I would bear it ? No, certainly I would not. I would throw down my musket saying let such as the Duke of Portland, who claims the country fight for it, for I am but as a stranger and sojourner and have neither part nor lot amongst them.* " [1]

No wonder Spence was advised to let judgment go by default !

Meantime, while Spence was still awaiting trial, the Committee presented its Second Report to Parliament (May 15th). The Second Report details the seditious practices alluded to in the First Report. It says that the political societies described in the 1799 Reports had never ceased their activities in London or in the country. Lancashire and Yorkshire were hotbeds of disaffection. In 1801, the Suspension Act having expired, those who had been detained in prison were released. This was the occasion of great rejoicing among their friends, and the political societies began to lift up their heads. One of these was a society

[1] The extracts are from the " Restorer," Letter I, pp. 20–1, Letter III, p. 23, Letter V, pp. 26–9, 31. This page is according to the second and non-phonetic edition of his " Trial " (1803 or 1807).

called " Spensonians," which was formed to discuss public affairs. The members agreed with a book published by Spence, who wished to exterminate royalty and nobility, to abolish private property and to carry an agrarian law " for the purpose of an equal parochial division of the profits of land as the basis of a beautiful and powerful new republic." This was to be effected " by a general insurrection of the people for which the revolutionary outrages in France and the mutiny in our fleet are held out as laudable examples." The members boasted of the extension of their Society, and at a supper given by them toasts of a treasonable nature were drunk. The Report then plunges into Irish affairs.

Place says that the appendix contained an address of Spence's and that extracts were given from his " Spensonia." [1]

Spence did not intend to miss the glorious opportunity which his trial provided of proclaiming his Plan and of suffering for it. He was tried by Lord Kenyon at Westminster Hall on May 27th. Judgment nearly did go by default, for the trial came on much sooner than he had expected. Luckily, he arrived early at the court, for he found that the trial had already begun. " His trial was set down as the fourth in the list for next day, he went by 8 o'clock in the morning as good luck would have it and the trial was *on*." [2] The *Morning Chronicle* says that Spence was charged with publishing a seditious libel, that some passages were read from his letter to the

[1] Place, 27808, p. 155.
[2] George Cullen's MS. note on the pamphlet " Important Trial " in the British Museum, 2nd edition, 1807, 900. 1. 2. (1).

people of Great Britain, and that nothing more was necessary. However, Spence thought differently, and his defence lasted for three hours.

The basic principle of this defence must be understood, otherwise Spence appears to be simply an ignorant and somewhat absurd fanatic. To publish such a book in time of war was inviting trouble, and he deserved punishment for this indiscretion. There could be no question that he did " publish and cause and procure to be published " the book in question, for he proudly admitted the fact. " Seditious libel " was a conveniently vague term used by the Government to comprehend much that would be regarded nowadays as merely hostile criticism. But the passages in the " Restorer " to which objection had been taken were not just hostile criticism of society or of the Government, though under ordinary circumstances they would probably have been ignored. Pitt, it seems, had been unwilling to proceed against Spence, on the ground that he was of little influence or importance.[1] Spence troubled himself little with the legal or with the temporal aspect of his case. He was concerned simply with the question of *Justice*. If he could prove his philanthropy and the excellency of his intentions, then, surely, it would be unjust to punish him. He must have felt, as the *Morning Chronicle* suggests, that he was a kind of Socrates.

He begins by expressing his astonishment at the Second Report. He says that to issue such a Report twelve days before his trial was, in effect, to prejudge him. He has always hoped for a millennium. His Plan

[1] Place, Add. MSS. 27808, p. 317.

is twenty-six years old, so that he was just as guilty twenty-six years ago when no attention was paid to him. He stands alone except for " a thinking few." He has no party and no money. He cannot even employ an attorney. He makes these statements in order to remove any prejudice that the Report might have created against him. To his mind, there is a radical injustice in trying him before jurors who are all men of property. Half the jury should be composed of labourers.

He cannot let justice go by default, although he has been advised to do so, for, " I stand here, gentlemen, in a singular case. Not as a mere bookseller, vending the works of others, or as a hireling supplying the views of any faction, but as an original legislator for having formed the most compact system of Society on the immovable basis of Nature and Justice, which no arguments can have power against as you will soon be convinced of." [1]

He then read the offending pamphlet, " The Restorer of Society to its Natural State," to the Court, with such comments as he deemed necessary by way of explanation or justification.

The title-page with its motto : " The Bold Political Innovator is probably as necessary a character as any other for the improvement of the world . . ." is, he holds, a sufficient justification for the work that follows. After the title-page come certain objections that had been made to his scheme together with his answers. These also he read. He made one comment which glances obliquely at the indictment—

[1] " Important Trial," p. 10.

his scheme will benefit the rich by depriving them of debilitating luxuries.   The letters which follow advocate various measures of public utility, such as the establishment of granaries and the provision of public bathing-places—proofs of his philanthropy.   A great part of them is devoted to his Plan.   He hopes to convince the Court of its merits, and so establish his claim to be praised, not punished.   Letter V had been quoted at length in the indictment.   Therefore he must explain it.   The mere reading would be insufficient to show that the indictment had misrepresented him in thus plucking passages from their context.   He tells the story of the Town-Moor contest, which took place in the days of his youth, in order to justify his statement that the Samsons must be scalped lest they pulled " the temple of liberty about our ears."

" It is impossible, gentlemen, for a poor man to enjoy equal rights in Society with Men of overgrown consolidated Estates." [1]   He does not know how he came to include royalty in his statement, " For ill-destroyed Royalty and Aristocracy will be sure to recover and overspread the Earth again."   Provided that his system is adopted, he has no objection to Kings.   He does not aim at inciting the King's liege subjects against him.   Sparta became a democracy and yet retained its Kings.[2]   As to his remarks about the fleet, the gentlemen of the jury must remember that the affair of the fleet has become an historical fact liable to be mentioned by the whole world, and likewise by posterity.   It is " bold reasoning " to

[1] " Important Trial," p. 27.   [2] Ibid., p. 28.

state that landsmen have more chance of mutinying successfully and have less to fear than seamen. But who is reasoning thus ? " And for what Purpose ? Why it is a legislator advocating the cause of the whole Human Race, whether now living, or that shall live, to the end of time. And, surely, it would not become a person engaged in so august a cause to be slavishly intimidated and write as if trembling for fear of paltry consequences." Besides, he is sounding no tocsin as a signal to massacre, for men will be swayed by the irresistible force of reason. They must be unanimous. " For, pray, gentlemen, who can suppose a few parishes to become so wise and so well instructed in their rights as to think of adopting my constitution without supposing the whole nation equally so, nay, one may say the whole world ? " [1]

He can hardly help laughing at the seriousness with which his " sylvan joke " of four and twenty years ago has been treated.[2]

He explains in the Letters what provision will be made, if his Plan is carried out, for those who lose their employment, the landlords, lawyers, and their servants, the soldiers and sailors. Those who lose land will be allowed to keep their furniture, pictures, clothes, jewellery and other movables. " This," he pointed out to the Court, " is not filling the hungry with good things and sending the Rich empty away." Some of the jury smiled at this observation.[3]

Judas bought land with the reward of iniquity. There has been too much bloodshed and too much

[1] " Important Trial," pp. 29–30.   [2] Ibid., p. 31.
[3] Ibid., p. 40.

iniquity in the acquisition of land.   Even in the days
of the Rechabites there was " engrossing " of land,
though it was not as bad then.   The Rechabites had
returned to a more primitive state of society because
they had not thought of dividing the rents.   They
could escape harpies, the lords of the manor, of those
times because there were still some waste places.
There is no place of retreat left now.   Preaching is no
use.   It is a good constitution and good laws that are
wanted.

After dealing with other details and advantages of
his scheme, he laments that in spite of his efforts to
make it well known and well understood many are
still ignorant about it.   But this is not surprising
when the avarice and selfishness of mankind are taken
into account.   His Letter proposing certain hospital
reforms, shows that he is not studying the " interests
of any particular set of men," but the public good.
It is a " sufficient defence for the whole book." [1]

He hopes that the jury is convinced of his upright
intentions.   " I was confirmed in my Proceedings by
the delectable Descriptions of earthly Felicity, figura-
tively set forth by the Prophets and Apostles, as
coming on the Earth in the latter days.   And I found
also as I proceeded, that the hopes of a future blessed
state arising from pure Justice was congenial to the
Ideas of all Men.   For religious People look for such
a state under the Notion of a Millennium, Philosophers
in an Age of Reason, and Poets in a future Golden
Age. . . . Now, Gentlemen, is it my Fault that any
class of men should be at variance with every picture

[1] " Important Trial," p. 53.

of Human Happiness ? Would it not be better to suppress the Bible than to suffer poor wretched creatures to delude themselves at the Hazard of Imprisonment with Hopes of Millenniums and New Jerusalem ? " [1]

Perhaps Judas would have been no traitor if there had been no land to buy. He wants to end " Judasism."

" Gentlemen, it is said that the State of the Damned is doubly miserable by being within sight of the blessedness of Heaven." [2]

A Plan is necessary to the Government, to trade, to soldiers, to sailors. Nations must have Plans, too. His book is a book of principles, which cannot be affected whatever may happen to him. He has restored order to language and politics. " Yet strange ! That for restoring order and justice, I should stand here in jeopardy of a prison." [3]

Having justified himself by reference to the Scriptures, he next turns to Locke.

He could not have lived in peace, he explains, with such truths secreted in his bosom. He is the " unfee'd Advocate of the disinherited seed of Adam." There never was a " trial of such magnitude " since the creation of the world. He has drawn up his Plan out of charity to the rich. He beseeches the jury to remember how Joseph had neglected his opportunity to befriend mankind and had become an oppressor. His posterity fell into the Pit [i.e. Slavery] that Joseph had escaped. The jury should take warning from this.

[1] " Important Trial," p. 57.   [2] Ibid., p. 59.   [3] Ibid.

If he is condemned, no one will dare to propose reforms. Besides, his book is just a "law unpassed."

At this point he read an extract from Priestly on the liberty of the Press.

Again he urged his innocency. His Plan was not lightly taken up. He has been working at it since 1775. He has discussed it with men of all ranks, and no one has ever accused him of evil intentions. Here follows the long extract from Harrington which he read to the jury. It is a defence of a man's right to publish his opinions. He ended with another extract on the liberty of the Press, this time from Lord Loughborough.

The *Morning Chronicle* corroborates the "Important Trial." It says that Spence read the "Restorer" through from beginning to end with comments, and that he did not deny but laboured to establish the truth and gloried in what he had done. He likened himself to Moses and the Prophets, to the Apostles and Martyrs who bled for the doctrines of Jesus, and particularly to Hampden, Sir Thomas More, and the great champions of British freedom. When he had concluded, Lord Kenyon observed that if any honest man could entertain a doubt in this case, all the arguments that he could use would not make it clear. The jury immediately found the prisoner guilty, and he was committed to Newgate. "The Bethlehem Hospital would certainly have been a better place," commented the *Chronicle*.

On June 13th Spence was brought to the Guildhall to receive judgment. Lord Kenyon asked him if he had anything to say. He vindicated all that he had done, and tried to persuade the Court that society would never be happy until his Plan was tried. He said that he had been misconstrued by the newspapers. He had been held up as a fool and a madman, and had been reported as likening himself to Moses, the Prophets, and the Apostles. Nothing could be more foolish or libellous " if such a person as I can be libelled. For your Lordships know that I only said that I wrote what I did with as good a conscience and as much philanthropy as any Prophet, Apostle, or Philosopher that ever existed." He knows what people think should be done with him. His opinions are treated with contempt, " as has hitherto been done with so much success, and this manner has been particularly practised by the most professed champions of Liberty." But only the hot-headed clamoured for vengeance. He admonished the judges, warning them what they must expect from posterity, to whom he looked for his reward, if they dealt with him harshly. If he was being punished so that no more theories of government might be written, it would be useless, as he had filled up the vacuum for such theories already.

He did not find men very grateful clients. He was " stung with the ingratitude of the present age." " For in the first place the people without [outside prison] treat me with the contempt due to a lunatic, for it is only the Government that wishes to make me appear as of consequence, and the people within treat me as bad or worse than the most notorious felon among them. And what with redeeming and ransoming my Toes from being pulled off with a string while in bed and paying heavy fines and manifold fees, there is no getting through the various impositions." [1]

"Now, my Lords, it is only in the Hope I entertain of the good system working reformation in the manners of the Human race that reconciles me to my task." [2]

On June 20th, after an admonitory harangue with Mr. Justice Grose, he was sentenced to be confined in Salop Gaol for twelve calendar months, to pay a fine of £20, and at the end of the period to give security in £500 for his good behaviour during the next five years. Presumably the fine was paid, as there were no further proceedings. At the end of the phonetic edition of his "Trial," a note states that he had printed it in phonetics as a token of gratitude to those who had helped him. Very likely Place came to his aid, as he did to Evans's.

The verdict was a foregone conclusion. Place thinks that the indictment should have been proved to the hilt by the Attorney-General. Had Spence been defended by a clever lawyer, his words might have been manipulated so as to render them less "seditious, malicious and scandalous" in sound. He might have played upon the feeling of compassion that there was for Spence and have made something out of the issue of the Second Report before the trial. He might, too, have worked up a defence from the fact that the title of the pamphlet was not given in the indictment, although the Attorney-General said that he was prosecuting Spence for the publication of the "Restorer." But Spence would have scorned lawyers' tricks, and perhaps the humble Socrates won more pity for himself than any lawyer could have done for him.[1]

Forlorn as Spence appeared to sympathizers like Cobbett, who was sufficiently interested to attend the trial, or like Place, who writes indignantly of his treatment, he was not alone. He had at least one faithful friend.

A MS. note on the title-page of his " Important Trial," signed " G. Cullen," says, " I am proud to say I was one of his bail, and when Sir Richard Ford asked me if I would be answerable for his appearance in such a sum (I forget now how much) I answered, ' Yes, in the ten thousands was I worth it ' . . . ! " This must be the " G. Cullen " of Knightsbridge, to whom Charles Hall sends his respects in a letter to Spence.[2]

At the actual trial " a friend of the philosopher, who had very much the appearance of one of his school, attempted to interpose in his favour, but silence was immediately imposed on him by the Court." He was a " crack-brained," half-witted organist. Was he " G. Cullen " ? [3]

A tract in the British Museum, Boulanger's " Christianity Unveiled," translated by W. M. Johnson, New York, 1795, evidently belonged to George Cullen, for it is liberally annotated by him. In one or two places

---

[1] Spence's trial is reported in the *Morning Chronicle* and in the *Annual Register*, June 13, 1801. But there appears to be no official record. It is ignored in the Reports of the King's Bench cases and in Howell's " State Trials."

[2] " Trial," British Museum, 2nd edition (1807), 900. 1. 2. (1). Place, 27808, p. 280. Charles Hall wrote in 1807.

[3] *Morning Chronicle, Annual Register*, June 13, 1801; *Newcastle Magazine*; Place, 2780, p. 303.

he has signed these MS. notes. His writing and spelling show that he was not cultured. On one page he writes : " I remember my mother whipping me for only asking the second time what God was. She was a Roman Catholic, and notwithstanding she was a very religious woman, she was almost always in poverty and trouble, and for many years I never missed a day but I went to church or chappel to worship God, and now I am convinced there is none." His annotations show that he was in search of truth, and that he had reached the stage when he could no longer accept what he had formerly held as truth. No fresh light had come to him. Perhaps light came to him from Spence.

CHAPTER VI

FRIENDS AND CONTEMPORARIES

SPENCE suffered, during his imprisonment, from insufficient food. On November 20, 1801, he wrote to Mr. Panther, a coach-builder in Oxford Street :—

SALOP GAOL,
MR. PANTHER. *Nov.* 20th, 1801.
SIR,

I beg pardon for thus troubling you, but I believe there are not many who in such a position as mine would conceal their case from their friends, for though there may be merit in suffering publicly, there can be none in private suffering. It can serve no purpose whatever, but is quite thrown away and lost. I have, therefore, written to two or three friends, informing them of my case, but have received no answers. My case, Sir, is that I have long been reduced to the bare gaol allowance, which is a small loaf of bread and an ounce of butter per day. Now I believe very few would think this sufficient aliment, especially when I assure you that I could eat a great deal more bread, if I had it. You may depend upon what I say because the Governor sees this letter and every letter which either goes from or comes to this place. If therefore you and a few other friends would send me a trifle to buy if it were but tea and sugar would very much oblige

Yours

If you direct for me at the gaol it will come safe to hand. I am well in health, thank God, though very thin in person. Please remember me to all inquiring friends.[1]

[1] Place, Add. MSS. 27808, p. 22. This letter, which is unsigned, may be only a copy, as it is written on the blank page of a proof sheet of his Bible.

In April of that year the Governor had written to ask if a better allowance could be made to the convicts, who fared worse then the felons. The felons' food was provided for them, but the "convicts" bought their own and were charged exorbitant prices. They paid sixpence for a ten-ounce loaf out of half a crown's weekly allowance.[1]

Spence relieved the tedium and hardship of his imprisonment by writing verses and devising new methods of making his Plan known.

One night as a slumb'ring I lay on my bed
A notable vision came into my head,
Methought I saw numbers forthgoing to teach
And Justice and Peace among Mankind to preach,
Saying, " Men mind your interest if you've common sense
And hearken to reason and friend Tommy Spence."

Or,

> One night on his bed
> It came into his head
>   While locked up in Shrewsbury jail,
> To send out Field Preachers
> And peaceable Teachers
>   With doctrines that never can fail.[2]

The letter to Mr. Panther is a further proof that Spence was not friendless. Probably his friends were too poor to help him much either in prison or out of it. He had determined to form these friends into a society for the propagation of his principles at least as early as 1801. Perhaps he had dreamt of forming one ever since his arrival in London. True, he had

[1] H.O. Papers, 61.
[2] Spence's "Songs," Part II; "Propagation of Spensonianism," written in Shrewsbury Gaol, 1801, etc.

denied the existence of a Spensonian Society in his defence, but he had circulated a bill which shows him proceeding to institute one.

LONDON, 18 MARCH, 1801.

AT A MEETING OF
REAL FRIENDS TO TRUTH AND JUSTICE
AND
HUMAN HAPPINESS

It was resolved that the principles of Citizen Spence's theory of Society are as inevitable and unchangeable as truth and nature on which they are built, and therefore only require universal investigation to be universally acknowledged. Resolved therefore that it be recommended to all the well-wishers to the system to meet frequently though in ever so small numbers in their respective neighbourhoods after a free and easy manner without encumbering themselves with rules to converse on the subject, provoke investigation, and answer real objections as may be stated, and to promote the circulation of Citizen Spence's publications. Resolved also that such convivial or free and easy meetings should assume some indications of their principles, such as Restorer of Society to its Natural State.[1]

From the Report it is fairly easy to see what was happening. There is no reason to doubt that at any given time Spence could count on three or four acquaintances to listen to him and to talk to their friends and neighbours about his doctrines. These would be " the thinking few." " The meeting of true friends " may have been composed of two or three individuals.

Spence's projected Society evidently had a fair chance of becoming a reality in 1801. Societies, prophesying a millennium, were fashionable just then

[1] Quoted by Place, 27808, p. 195.

among certain sections of the people, and though the
Spensonians were not religious enthusiasts like the
Jerusalemites, they came in for a share of popularity,
and they benefited also from the encouragement given
by the leaders of other societies on their release from
prison.

Thomas Evans was released in 1801. It must have
been then that he began to turn his attention
from the United Englishmen to the Spensonians.
He would be one of the "old leaders" who were
encouraging Spence and his followers. He settled
down to his brace-making, and in 1805 went to live
in Newcastle Street, Strand.

The arrest and imprisonment of Spence frustrated
the efforts of the Spensonians for the time being.

Whether Spence's scheme of sending out field
preachers materialized, it is impossible to say, as
Spence says nothing more about them and they did
not make themselves notorious.

By 1807 a Society was actually in existence.

At the sign of the Fleece, Little Windmill Street, the Free
and Easy meets every Tuesday at eight o'clock. For a
"trifle apiece."
Spence treats all the swine with a jest.[1]

At these meetings questions were debated, Spence's
Plan discussed, and his pamphlets offered for sale.
The meeting ended with song, jest and drink. The
Society had its Song-book containing the verses of
Spence, Evans, and one or two other disciples.

Evans supplied the "Humourous Catalogue of

[1] "Humourous Catalogue of Spence's Songs," inserted in the
two collections of his "Songs." In the original Tuesday has been
crossed out and altered to "Monday."

Spence's Songs." At one meeting he read his poem "An Address to Posterity Warning them against the Landlord Judas." Then he sat down and wrote another poem, "The Touchstone of Honesty," which was sung to the tune "Lillibullera." Another of his songs, "Address to the Fair," called on the ladies to assist in the good cause. "The Inefficacy of the French Revolution" was sung to "Malbrouck."

> The Gallic Revolution
> Pretended Restitution
> But where's their distribution
> On the Agrarian Plan ?
> They wanted Tommy Spence
> To teach them common sense.

Or they sang :—

> For Man to be happy and social and free
> The land must possess and as brothers agree
> The profits to share and the rents to divide
> Then fight for't they will if they come to be try'd.
> Tol de Rol. . . .

> If the Rights of Men were established on Earth
> No more then of slaughter, oppression or dearth,
> To do it is wanting but plain common sense,
> 'Tis printed and published by good Tommy Spence.
> Tol de Rol. . . .

> [See "Constitution of Spensonia."]

Another member, Mr. W. Tilly, contributed "The Spencean Jubilee."

It is evident from the two collections of Songs that Evans played a leading part in the Society.

Probably the "Humourous Catalogue," Spence's broadsides, "Rights of Man in Verse," "An Infallible

Way to make Peace," " An Infallible Way to Make Trade," and occasional poems, would be distributed gratis or sold for a small price at the meeting.   Parts I and II of the " Songs " were sold for one penny each.

Hone describes how Spence advertised his Plan and canvassed for his Society.   He says : " I saw Spence with his ' vehicle ' and bought his ' Trial ' from it in Parliament Street, near the ' Duke of Richmond's.' My personal intercourse with him was very little, for I disliked his manner, but I was a frequent observer of him on account of his fearless thinking and printing. About 1808–09 he came to the Strand for one of Sir F. Burdett's speeches, and talked away about his Plan and the Landlords against whom he was inveterate. On leaving he gave me a card (long since lost) admitting the bearer to a meeting at the *Something* and Lamb, in or near Windmill Street, where he said he met his friends to talk over and co-operate towards his Plan. I should not have objected to going there as a spectator, but I knew that could not be and therefore did not go. . . . His ' vehicle ' . . . was very like a baker's close barrow, the pamphlets were exhibited outside, and when he sold one he took it from within, and handed and recommended others with strong expressions of hate to the powers that were, and prophecies of what should happen to the whole race of ' Landlords.' " [1]

Spence's song, " Spence and the Barber," described him in the act of canvassing.   It relates how a Barber complained to Spence that he could hardly manage

[1] Quoted by Professor Graham Wallas, " Life of Place," p. 69. Place, 27808, p. 314.

to live, rents and taxes were so high, food and clothes
so expensive.

> Cheer up, man, said Spence, never fear
> You soon will have my Constitution.

The Barber " flew in a rage," it was " too wicked
an age " to have justice.

> Said Spence, if a few hearty men
> Said, Come let us have Spence's System.
> What would your behaviour be then,
> Would you hinder, or would you assist 'em ?

Spence explains to the Barber that his interest is
that of nine-tenths of the nation—and thereby secures
a promise of assistance from the Barber. He is
willing to assist the nine-tenths !

Evans tried to convert a police officer who owned
the land on which his public-house was built. He
assured him that if the Spencean system were adopted,
he as landlord would pay £40 to the parish for his
land and would have nothing more to pay as rates
or taxes. This would save him £100 a year !

As usual, Spence resorted to chalking inscriptions
on walls. Lord Sidmouth was growing uneasy in 1812
about these notices and the sale of Spence's literature
in the streets. The inscriptions brought at least one
convert. A Mr. Porter in a long poem, " Spence's
Plan " (Tune : " Poor Jack "), narrates :—

> As I went forth one morn
> For some recreation
> My thoughts did quickly turn
> Upon a Reformation.
> But far I had not gone
> Or could my thoughts recall, sir,
> Ere I spied Spence's Plan
> Wrote up against a wall, sir.

> I star'd with open eyes
> And wondered what it meant, sir,
> But found with great surprise
> As farther on I went, sir,
> Dispute it if you can
> I spied within a lane, sir,
> Spence's " Rights of Man "
> Wrote boldly up again, sir.
>
> Determined in my mind
> For to read his Plan, sir,
> I quickly went to find
> This enterprising man, sir.
> To the Swan I took my flight
> Down in the New Street Square, sir,
> Where every Monday night
> Friend Tommy Spence comes there, sir.[1]

.   .   .   .   .

Four more verses follow in which Mr. Porter sets forth how he bought a book and learnt about parochial ownership of the land and other Spencean doctrines.

This pleasant piece of autobiography unfortunately tells us little of Mr. Porter and his associates personally. It has been possible, however, to glean some meagre information of other attendants at Spencean meetings. Place surely must have attended an occasional meeting, though his silence on the subject might be taken to infer that, like Hone, his caution outweighed his curiosity. Galloway certainly attended. When Spence died he gave an order to Edwards (the spy) for fifteen busts of the reformer. It was probably Galloway who introduced his friend Robert Moggridge.[2] Moggridge became a frequenter of the Society,

---

[1] Slip inserted in the Goldsmith edition of the " Important Trial," 2nd edition, 1807, A. 07. 4.

[2] His name and address are in the list Place made of Spence's friends. Place obtained his copy of the " Restorer " from him. " R. Moggridge " is written in ink on the pamphlet. Place says nothing of him, but vide H.O., 40. 5.

and, in 1817, he was arrested for attempting to help Thistlewood escape from the country. Robert Wedderburn told Place that he learnt about the order of the busts from Edwards. He said that he himself knew Spence nine months before his death. Wedderburn was a writer of pamphlets, one of which, the " Axe Laid to the Root of the Tree," had but an indifferent sale.[1]

Place has made a list of eight people to whom he intended to apply for information about Spence. Three of these, Savage, an undertaker, Dennison, and Fair, figure inconspicuously at the time of the Spa-Field Riots. One is " Mrs. Seale, St. Pancras Workhouse." Seale and Bates were Spence's printers.[2]

An account of Spence's personal friends and acquaintances must include some reference to Allen Davenport, " Poet and Publicist," as his biographer [3] magniloquently terms him. He first knew Spence in 1804, and was a Spencean until his death in 1847. He was a self-made man, of lowly birth and mediocre talents, who wrote a good many verses, pamphlets, and newspaper articles. Spence appears to have inspired in him, as in Thomas Evans, both veneration and affection. He died in great poverty without leaving anything to pay his funeral expenses, except a pamphlet he had just written; yet, to judge from the numbers who attended his funeral, he was a man much respected.

The Society was also joined by the two Watsons, father and son, profligate apothecaries driven crazy

[1] H.O., 40. 7. Place, Add. MSS. 27808, p. 322.
[2] Place, Add. MSS., p. 139.   [3] Holyoake.

by poverty. Preston was another prominent member. " Preston was also wretchedly poor. He was one of those singular characters to whom poverty can hardly be said to be a misfortune. He was proud of his own knowledge, fond of displaying it, and cared for little beyond food and rags when by talking nonsense he could attract the attention of two or three men as ignorant as himself. He was a small man, lame in one foot." [1]

The Watsons and Preston were Spenceans who wanted to establish the Plan by a revolution. They were encouraged and led by Arthur Thistlewood, gentleman. He was a reckless ne'er-do-well and gambler who was determined " to do something." He aspired to play the part of Cataline, but he lacked Cataline's brain and was as foolish as he was reckless.

In Spence's time the Society was simply a club of poor workmen anxious to improve the world in general and their own condition in particular. Naturally it attracted a few of the more imprudent who might easily be led to commit violent and foolish acts if temptation came their way—as it did. No doubt, as Place says, the majority of them had little understanding of the doctrines they sought to propagate.

Spence passed the remainder of his life, 1801–14, in obscurity. He published little, though he continued to issue broadsides and to sell pamphlets. The times were no longer propitious for reformers, he was very poor, and he was probably basing more hopes upon his disciples than on his pamphlets. He had quitted his shop in Oxford Street before his trial. Place says

[1] Place, 27809, p. 72.

that he " was driven from his little shop." [1] On the back of the last page of the " Restorer " (1801), T. Spence of " Number 3 Great Castle Street, Oxford Market " announces that he keeps a bookstall near the Pantheon, Oxford Street. On the broadsides published after his release he subscribes himself, " T. Spence, number-carrier and bookbinder, 15 Princes Street, Soho."

Place has preserved part of a correspondence, belonging to the year 1807, between Spence and Charles Hall. Charles Hall of Tavistock was a physician who had published an essay, " Effects of Civilization on the People of Europe," in 1805. Like Spence, he believed that to allow private property in land was neither just nor expedient. Disease and mortality, he said, were due to lack of food consequent upon an insufficient cultivation of the land. The land was insufficiently cultivated because labour was diverted to the manufacture of luxuries. The poor do not have a fair share of their produce. Eight-tenths of the people consume only one-eighth of the produce of labour. He would have an equal distribution of wealth [= landed property]. A man should enjoy the whole fruits of his labour, and he ought to work one-third or one-fourth of his present time. Men can produce most of what they need except " Materia Medica," and that they are as well without. He would forbid " refined manufactures." Every man

---

[1] A MS. note on a copy of the " End of Oppression " in the British Museum, 1389, C.12.3, says that Spence " kept a book-shop in Oxford Street, near St. Giles, and afterwards a stall near the Pantheon, whither he conveyed his stock every morning in a sort of caravan."

ought to be engaged in productive labour [= agriculture], but a few men might be selected to devote themselves to the arts and sciences.

Writing from Tavistock, June 9, 1807, Hall says that he has not so far given Spence an opinion of his [Spence's] work, as he did not know whether Spence had asked for it " with a view of publishing a new edition." " But I now suppose that you have no such intention. I shall therefore only make some general remarks. The first is that I cannot conceive what should induce you to disguise your work with such a whimsical kind of spelling which renders it so difficult to read, that I could more easily read a book in four or five dead or foreign languages than I could read yours in my native tongue. You say that it is not formed from mere vulgar and uncertain sound, but is systematic, but to acquire a system so as to use it readily requires too much time for the reading a single work. Was it not for this disguise, I think your language clear, concise and correct, and that you put things in a true, strong light. In some passages you show a considerable degree of humour. I think your defence manly and eloquent. It is unnecessary to say that I approve your sentiments, since as you observe they are so much like my own.

" You say that communications between the well-wishers of the people might be beneficial to them. The only way that individuals like you and I can be of use to them is by convincing both the rich and the poor, that the evils of the latter are the direct and necessary effect of the system of civilization and not those of human nature and the condition of human affairs—as the rich and parsons in particular endeavour to persuade them." [1]

The two succeeding letters, one from Spence and one from Hall, are missing. The next is from Spence to Hall. He is sorry that they cannot agree better. Authors ought to have some definite plan on which they are agreed, and then something could be done. He is certain of his own Plan :—

"I think, Sir, you do not rightly understand me or you would see plainly that all the good you aim at is fully comprehended in my plan. It is strange you should think the farmers would become so rich and powerful in such a free and well-regulated state as to swallow up the poor. You forget that these farmers pay their Rents to those very Poor, that all farms are let by auction for the highest Rent they will bring and that in the case of insufficiency of vacant lands to supply all the People inclined to go over to Agriculture the great Farms would be broke down into small allotments to answer the Demands. . . . You seem to be sliding into the system of Sir Thomas More's 'Utopia' wherein he makes every kind of property the property of the nation and the People obliged to work under gang-masters as you hint at. But I do not think you will find many willing to go into such a state of Barbarism and Slavery. Good God! Would you have us all to become again Goths and Vandals and give up every elegant comfort

[1] For this correspondence, vide Place, Add. MSS., 27808, p. 280 : 3rd letter, June 1, 1807, Hall to Spence ; 6th letter, June 28, 1807, Spence to Hall ; 7th letter, August 13, 1807, Spence to Hall (publications enclosed) ; 8th letter, August 25, 1807, Hall thanks Spence for " Pigs' Meat," etc.

of life ? But we may rest contented that this can never be without another universal Deluge. . . ."

Hall did not reply to this, so Spence wrote to apologize for any offence he may have given. He sent Hall some of his publications—" Pigs' Meat "—and Hall replied :—

" But the point you wish me to speak to. I have said before that it is the part of the subject I have least thought of. My thoughts therefore can neither be deep nor new. I think what we should each aim at would be to go back a good way towards our natural state, to that point from which we strayed, retaining but little of that only (to wit of the coarser arts) which civilization has produced, together with certain sciences . . . when people became more numerous so as to require all the land in the then known method of agriculture to support them, they divided the lands, not letting one person have more than another. To this state we should return as being the most natural and simple. . . . Your plan seems to me to be too complicated. You would retain all the individual property except, as you imagine, that of the land. Among this is the live and dead stock of the land. . . . These are at present in very different proportions in different people's lands. Wealth would, therefore, remain still very unequal. This wealth (I mean individual) being power it would thus, as it is now, be exercised by the possessors over the non-possessors. The present system of society by the wicked custom of money, public debt, etc., is so complicated that we can hardly reduce one political phenomenon to its cause, so you by retaining much of this system cannot see what effects your plan would have. They would, I think, be very different from what you expect. You mean to establish an equality as to real property, i.e. land. But I doubt exceedingly whether you would effect what you intend. The nature of all property is so very abstract that I believe we know but little of it. I have suspected that those persons who receive the rent are only in part the owners of it, the tradesmen who furnish the landlord with drapery, cakes, goods, etc., etc., have all a claim a certain property (somewhat in the nature of a mortgage) on the land—the land here is the only real property as it is called in law—and all personal property is only property as it gives a right to a share in the land. You leave all this personal property untouched, and consequently, if my suspicions are just, the landed property is only partially divided. . . ."

Hall then goes on to explain that he is still considering the nature of material and immaterial property. Till the subject is understood no system of unequal property can be " pronounced with certainty to be salutary." He thinks, " as Moses seems to have done," that the accumulation of personal property should be prevented, especially when " personal property " includes the necessities of life. On these grounds he prefers his own Plan to that of Spence, and thinks it more suited " to our present imperfect state of political knowledge." Also it is safer.

He tells Spence in this letter that he is a widower nearly seventy years of age. He has eight sons and two daughters all grown up. He finds his practice very fatiguing owing to the long rides. He has difficulty in selling his pamphlets and is not well off. He asks Spence next time he sends him any books to send them to Messrs. Longman and Company, Paternoster Row, to be sent with the books for a bookseller at Tavistock. He is " charged 5/4d. by the coach for the least parcel." He is thinking of coming up to London, and wonders if Spence could recommend him suitable lodgings. He sends his respects to Mr. G. Cullen of Knightsbridge.

Soon after this he fell into debt through a lawsuit and he was imprisoned in the Fleet. His friends would have discharged the debts, but he would not allow this as he felt that the debts were not fairly owing. John Minter Morgan used to visit him in prison. He died there, aged eighty.

Charles Hall is an extreme reactionary. Both he and Spence see the weak spot in one another's plans, though mutual criticism would appear to have benefited neither. Hall misunderstands Spence when he interprets him as aiming at establishing equality of real property. But he was right when he said that the transfer of the landed property and the rents would be a much more complicated process than Spence supposed. The disposal of the live stock would entail some knotty problems.

Spence complained that he was treated with neglect and contempt, but he need not have complained. His numerous prosecutions, the attention the Government paid to him in 1801,[1] and his famous trial

[1] Certain passages in a copy of his " End of Oppression " have been marked as " cited by Lord Mornington in the House of

should have reassured him on that point. His early troubles, 1792–93, received due notice in the papers. The reference in them to Spence as the " Poor Pamphleteer " proves that locally he was a public figure, and suggests that he was regarded with some amount of interest or curiosity. The brevity of the cuttings is no disparagement. Newspapers then had little space even for exalted personages. The *Morning Chronicle* gives quite a long account of the trial in 1801. It is true that the paper advocates Bedlam for him, but the space given to the trial and the detail of the report betokens an interest in the proceedings on the part of the readers of the *Chronicle*, as well as on that of the reporter. Southey and Cobbett both bear witness to the interest and compassion excited by the trial.

He suffered plenty of abuse, and that in itself proves that he was not ignored.

Two letters, one published by Spence himself in the " Fragment of an Ancient Prophecy," the other kept by Place, describe the feelings that he excited in some loyal breasts.

TRUE COPY OF A LETTER TO THE PUBLISHER [= SPENCE].

MR. SPENCE,

I bought at your shop a few days back, a book entitled the " End of Oppression " which I conceive to be the basest book that ever was printed and as a Fellow Citizen I advise

---

Commons." See the British Museum copy of the pamphlet, 1389, C.12.3. This would be in 1817, after his death.

A note in the same handwriting states : " This poor deluded fellow after being repeatedly imprisoned and discharged kept a book-shop in Oxford Street . . . but still indulging his propensity for political satire he was taken into custody. . . ."

you to stop the sale of it, or otherwise I hope your book will be publicly burnt and you yourself hanged for you richly deserve it.

A DEMOCRAT.

May 17th, 1796.

MR. SPENCE,

I have looked at your book and Tryal. I believe God in mercy to the Nation will prevent your wild plan from taking place. A more ridiculous and wicked system I think I never met with. You advise robbery in the first act which would lead your party on to murder, for there is not an honest man in the country but would resist your wickedness. You have read the Bible until you are as blind as one without eyes and literally so. It is God who putteth up one, and putteth down another. Afflictions do not spring out of the ground nor troubles rise by chance, but you talk of putting up or putting down. I believe there is not a discerning man in the kingdom but is persuaded your notions are from the Devil himself. You have had great lenity shown you, instead of one year perhaps none would have repined if it had been for life. Your incoherent notions are pregnant with vast mischief and destruction, lett me advise you to burn all the books you have left and never open your mouth about them again, attend only to your business and leave Politicks. If you go on, be assured you will end at last in destruction both to body and soul.

Yours &c.,

27 July, 1808.   THOS. CONSTABLE.

His exploits as a token-dealer brought him notoriety and won him a conspicuous place in the *Gentleman's Magazine* for 1797–98. The anger of the magazine writers was in part due to Spence's political activities.

Spence told the Court in 1801 that he had discussed his Plan with people of all classes, from Church dignitaries and Members of Parliament down to labourers. Hence the conversations and arguments in his pamphlets.

Thomas Evans, writing in 1821, said that it was then very difficult to obtain any of Spence's tracts. He supposed that wealthy people bought them up. The tracts in the British Museum and the Goldsmiths' Library have been acquired for the most part from private collectors. They must have been regarded at least as " curios," or they would not have been preserved. Judging from Place and from the correspondence with Hone on the subject, they evidently were regarded as remarkable, so that the opinion of Thomas Evans may be correct, and Spence may have had a reading public in the very people who treated him personally with contempt.

A good guide to public opinion would be a knowledge of the extent to which his pamphlets circulated. Several of them ran into two or more editions. Unfortunately there is little information to be gleaned. The *Morning Post* (December 1794) and the *Morning Chronicle* (January 1795) both inserted his letters advertising " Pigs' Meat." He says here and in the " Restorer " that many thousands had read the publication. There is every reason to believe that he did enjoy a brief popularity. His broadside " Rights of Man in Verse " sold at the rate of at least fifty to a hundred a day for a few weeks in 1797. As must be the case of all authors, and particularly of writers on political subjects, the sale of his pamphlets must have fluctuated considerably. The distress and the excitement in the country would give him a vogue in 1793, 1794, and 1797.[1]

[1] Vide Appendix, p. 248.

Place, Cobbett, and Hone [1] were all interested in Spence and his Plan.   Place intended to write a biography of the reformer.   Cobbett attended his trial in 1801, and found space for an account of Spence and the Spenceans in his " Twopenny Trash."   Hone was personally acquainted with Spence, and though he did not like him, read his pamphlets and desired to go to his meetings.   Later he befriended Evans and published accounts of the Spenceans and their persecutions.   Coleridge thought that the poor Spenceans possessed " half the truth," [2] while Malthus, noticing how Spenceanism had spread, remarks : " It is also generally known that an idea has lately prevailed among the lower classes of society that the land is the people's farm, the rent of which ought to be divided equally among them ; and that they have been deprived of the benefits which belong to them, from this their natural inheritance, and by the injustice and oppression of their stewards, the landlords." [3] He takes the trouble to point out in a special note that the Spenceans have estimated the gross rent of the United Kingdom at far too high a figure.[4]

But the most striking tribute was paid to Spence by Southey.   Southey, from being a revolutionary and a pantisocrat,[5] became the upholder of the Govern-

[1] Cobbett, *Weekly Register*, December 14, 1816, col. 633.   Hone, Letter to Place. Place, 27807, p. 314. Also Hone's Broadsheets, 1816.

[2] Coleridge, " Biographia Literaria," 1905. " Lay Sermons," p. 439.

[3] Malthus, " Essay on Population," 5th edition, 1817, pp. 273-4.

[4] Ibid., p. 280, note. Malthus is here referring to the calculation of Thomas Spence in " Christian Policy the Salvation of the Empire," 1816.

[5] The Pantisocrats were young men who dreamt of emigrating to South America, there to form a society in accordance with the principles enunciated by Godwin in his " Political Justice."

ment, of the ultra-Tories against their Radical and Whig enemies. He retained some of his earlier convictions. He was, for instance, keenly interested in the schemes of Robert Owen and withdrew his support of them on religious grounds alone.[1] Southey supported the Government by writing articles for the *Quarterly*, the Tory organ run in opposition to the *Edinburgh Review*. One of these articles, "On the State of Public Opinion and the Political Reformers," appeared anonymously in 1817.[2] In this essay he upholds the Government for attacking the reformers and justifies its severity. He doubts whether the various parties who clamour for parliamentary reform would be satisfied if they had it. Even if they were satisfied, there still remain the Spencean philanthropists. He then justifies the persecution of the sect. "A set of men not to be confounded with any of whom we have hitherto spoken," but "men who know distinctly what they mean and tell us honestly what they aim at, infinitely more respectable than the shallow orators who declaim about reform . . . and far more dangerous . . . as great and important truths half understood and misapplied are of all means of mischief the most formidable."

Southey really believed that the Spenceans had influence and that Spenceanism was a force, a force generated from truth and strengthened by the sincerity of the Spenceans. "Neither is the agrarian scheme

[1] Owen startled his sympathizers by announcing his views on religion at a public meeting in 1819. Vide his "Peace on Earth" pamphlets, 1817.

[2] It is included in the two volumes of Southey's Essays, published in 1832. Vide vol. i, p. 399, for the section on the Spenceans.

so foolish or so devoid of attractions that it may be safely despised."

" Divested of such nonsensical language which was then in full vogue [i.e. when Spence wrote] his scheme is that the soil belongs to the state and that individuals should rent their land . . . from their respective parishes . . . every kind of private property being permitted except in land."

Southey derived his knowledge of Spenceanism from Evans's " Christian Policy the Salvation of the Empire " and from Spence's " Important Trial." He is very complimentary to Spence. He notes the compassion that the " wretched and miserable fanatic excited," " for the man was honest, he was not one of those demagogues who like to make mischief their trade because they find it a gainful one." In his simple statements of the torments that he has endured in prison, he excuses the keeper, saying that these things were unknown to him. It was " fortunate that this man was not a religious as well as a political enthusiast." He was " poor and despised but not despicable, for he was sincere, stoical, persevering, single-minded and self-approv'd." The writer even adds that St. Francis of Assisi and Loyola were successful in times less favourable to their projects and with less alluring doctrines.

Spence would have rejoiced in such words as these from one of the " thinking few."

The uneasiness of Lord Sidmouth in 1812,[1] at the

---

[1] H.O., 65. 1 and 2. Lord Sidmouth in a circular letter to the police calls attention to the street literature and to the chalking of " improper inscriptions," " Spence's Plan and full bellies."

new outbreak of Spencean inscriptions, marks the emergence of Spence from his obscurity.   The Luddite riots and the general unrest in the country led the old reformer to think that a fresh opportunity to make his Plan known had arrived.   His Society increased in numbers, it was reorganized, and constituted formally as the Society of Spencean Philanthropists.   In August 1814 Spence began to publish a periodical called the *Giant-Killer or Anti-Landlord*.

Three numbers only of the new periodical had appeared when Spence was seized with a bowel complaint from which he died September 1, 1814.   In accordance with his wishes, his favourite coins, the " Cat " and the " Meridian Sun," were placed in his coffin.   Forty friends attended the funeral, which took place in the burial-ground of St. James's, Hampstead Road.   The funeral procession made its way up Tottenham Court Road.   A pair of scales draped in white ribbons and with an equal quantity of earth in each balance, to symbolize his innocence and the justice of his views, preceded his corpse.   Appropriate medallions were distributed among the crowd, and at the grave William Snow, one of his followers, made an oration.[1]

---

[1] A. Waters, " Trial of T. Spence," gives a copy of an entry from a register of St. James's, Piccadilly : " P. 240. Burials. In the Parish of St. James, Westminster, in the County of Middlesex—

Name.	Abode.	When buried.	Age.	By whom Ceremony performed.
No. 934 Thomas Spence	Castle St.	Sept. 8	63	J. Armstrong."

Waters concludes from this and the absence of any such entry in the registers of Whitefields Chapel, that the " New Burial Ground " was St. James's, Hampstead Road.

His death brought him once more before the public—
the busy world paused to pay tribute to the " Poor
Pamphleteer." The *Morning Post* of September 10th
announced his death, and in a long paragraph gave
an epitome of his Plan, made some complimentary
remarks on his personal character, and described the
funeral ceremonies. The *Courier* followed suit two
days later with a condensed version of the paragraph
in the *Post*. The *Gentleman's Magazine* for September
announced his death in a paragraph similar to that
of the *Courier*, but in March 1815 it gave the *Post's*
account in full. " He devised and published a Plan
by which all human-kind could be provided with
sustinence without pauperism. His writings are truly
singular and evince a most disinterested desire to serve
mankind."

In Newcastle itself, where one would expect a
special interest to be taken in Spence, special accounts
of him were published by Mackenzie, Sykes, Mitchell,
and Bewick.

So Spence died, leaving nothing to his friends but
" an injunction to promote his Plan, and the remembrance of his inflexible integrity." [1]

[1] Hone, "Broadsheets," 3, 1816. Place, Journals, 39, 1811–18,
p. 107.

CHAPTER VII

THE SPENCEAN PHILANTHROPISTS

SPENCE's injunctions to promote his Plan were faithfully carried out by Thomas Evans. In October 1814 he instituted the Society of Spencean Philanthropists. The distress in town and country of which the Luddite riots were symptomatic had strengthened the demand for reform and had led to the foundation of new political societies. The Hampden Clubs, founded under the leadership of old Major Cartwright and encouraged by such notable reformers as Sir Francis Burdett, were founded in 1814. Since 1812 the Spenceans had become increasingly active. Probably their numbers grew after the outbreak of the Luddite riots, and this must have encouraged Spence to make his Society more formal. The Society instituted by Evans would appear to have been a remodelled Spensonian Society. Its aims, methods and organization are described in one of its handbills.

Spence's Plan
For parochial Partnerships in the land
Is the only effectual remedy for the
Distresses and oppression of the People.
The Landholders are not Proprietors in chief, they are but
stewards of the Public
For the Land is the People's Farm.

The expenses of the Government do not cause the misery
that surrounds us, but the enormous exactions of these unjust
stewards.

Land monopoly is indeed equally contrary to the benign
spirit of

Christianity and destructive of the independence and morality
of mankind.

The Profit of the Earth is for all,

Yet how deplorably destitute are the mass of the People,

Nor is it possible for their situation to be radically amended but

By the establishment of a system, Founded on the immutable
basis of Nature and Justice

Experience demonstrates its necessity and the Rights of
Mankind require it for their preservation.

To obtain this important object by extending the knowledge
Of the above System, the Society of Spencean Philanthropists
has been instituted. Further information of its principles
may be obtained by attending any of its sectional meetings
where subjects are discussed calculated to enlighten the
human understanding and where also the regulations of the
Society may be procured containing a complete development
of the Spencean System. Every individual is admitted free
of expense who will conduct himself with decorum. The
meetings of the Society begin at a quarter after eight in the
evening as under.

First Section.	Every Wednesday	Cock, Grafton St., Soho.
Second Section.	Every Thursday	Mulberry Tree, Moorfields.
Third Section.	Every Monday	Nag's Head, Carnaby Market.
Fourth Section.	Every Tuesday	No. 8 Lumber St., Mint, Borough.

∴ Read " Christian Policy the Salvation of the Empire."
Price one shilling and sixpence.

Evans declared that only one Society of Spenceans
was founded, and that apart from the four sections
into which it was divided there were no branches.
The fact that there were four sections, each with its

special headquarters, shows that he was organizing the Society on the lines of the London Corresponding Society. He said that the meetings were freely and openly advertised, but that except for two or three private letters the Society carried on no correspondence.[1]

The Society, like other political societies of the time, was closely watched by the Government.

" Even the poor harmless Spenceans with their Library, consisting of an old Bible and three or four publications, a high priest under the Title of Librarian [Evans] and some forty or fifty followers were held out as bugbears to men of landed property." " Evans, the leader and master of the society, but in truth it could not be called a society, like all fanatics thought that he could produce a millennium." He used to march from his house to the public-house where the meeting was being held with an old Bible under his arm and preach from it to whoever would hear him.

" The Spenceans were next to nobody and nothing, they were as simple as harmless, and as harmless as simple." Their Society consisted of Evans, his son and their friends.[2]

The information of the spies give some detailed descriptions of the activities of Evans and his colleagues.[3]

January 20, 1816.—There were thirty or more Spenceans at the " Spotted Dog." Dr. Watson was

---

[1] Vide Petition, February 28, 1817 (Hansard).
[2] Place, 27809, pp. 33, 99, 100.
[3] This information is in the H.O. Papers, 40. 3. 4 and 7.

in the chair. There were more gentlemen there than usual.

November 15, 1816.—James Hanley of No. 11 White Cross Street, says that he attended a meeting at the "Mulberry Tree." . . . The chairman was named Savage. Anyone is admitted. There is a "conservative" committee,[1] composed of two deputies from each section, but he does not know where it is held. He held some private conversation with old Evans as to the Spa Fields Plans.

January ? 1817.—Mr. Clarke, Compasses, King Street, Golden Square, and Foy the officer were present at a meeting held at the "Nag's Head," Carnaby Market. There were fifty people present. A man of the name of Evans stated that the land was the People's Right. He asked everyone present if he agreed. Each answered "Yes," upon his honour, paid one shilling for printing expenses and received a card of membership. Mr. Evans stated that reform was a farce, it did not go far enough. A revolution was necessary.

February 6, 1817.—The Spenceans met at the "Mulberry Tree" to the number of 130 and upwards. Young Evans noticed in his speech that gentlemen were often asking how their Plan was to be put into execution. It was wrong, but he would answer once for all, "We cannot, we dare not tell." He hoped to hear no more of the matter. "We are too well aware of the admirable system of the present Government to hazard a prison or our lives." Old Watson

---

[1] The "conservative" committee was a secret committee which acted as the mainspring to the whole.

did not attend, nor did Preston. Pember was chairman, Edwards [the spy who worked up the Cato Street Conspiracy] was secretary.

October 1817.—Twenty Spenceans at the " Spotted Dog." Preston and forty others at the " Knave of Clubs."

November 13, 1817.—Informer " H " reports that a Polemic Society assembled at the " Mulberry Tree." Wedderburn, a noted Spencean, was active there. Pamphlets were on sale. The Society promoted atheism [a reference to such religious doctrines as those of Evans]. One member said that the Government was more annoyed with their Society than with any other. The question of better representation in town and country was debated. The next question was to be the " propriety of paying tithes." Then followed readings from Sherwin, Cobbett, and Wooller. The room was crowded to suffocation. It would hold one hundred with ease on debating nights.

Information was given respecting meetings of various societies. Sifting this out, the authorities found that the principal meetings of the lower classes were those held by the Spenceans at their four centres, while the " middling classes " held their meetings at three other public-houses. The meetings at the latter were chiefly to hear Cobbett's *Register*. Many meetings also took place to obtain signatures to petitions for parliamentary reform.

The lower and middle class meetings began about eight o'clock. Cobbett's *Register* was read on Sunday evening, and was followed by readings from the *Examiner* and the *Independent Whig*.

Other political tracts calculated to influence the un-thinking were also read. A reader was selected who stood at a desk. There was little argument. Such comments as the reader made were shaped according to his company. Debates soon deviated from the question and took to violent invective against the Ministers, Parliament, and every part of the Govern-ment. Dangerous suggestions of reform were made, such as annual elections, voting by ballot, universal suffrage, elective monarchies. Reform was said to be of no use while George Guelph was on the throne. There was a disposition for members to become disciples of the wildest and wickedest theories that ever destroyed the happiness of civil society. Meetings were attended by vendors of pamphlets who brought them for sale. The numbers attending the meetings varied from ¬ixty to a hundred. At the " Mulberry Tree " they numbered one hundred and fifty. The landlords of these houses were in sympathy with their customers. They signalled to the speaker if strangers appeared, then the subject of spies was started and violent threats were uttered as to the way they would be treated if they were caught. Those attending the meetings were very poor, yet there seemed to be no lack of funds which were used to hire men for their purposes at Spa˙ Fields [i.e. sandwichmen]. The meeting did not break up until 1 a.m.

Evans, then, was the librarian of the Spencean Society ; Hooper, one of the Spa Field rioters and a " remarkably poor imbecile creature," the treasurer; while Preston and George Edwards, a spy, both served in the capacity of secretary. A chairman was elected at each meeting. Evans and his friends fraternized with Watson, Hooper, Preston, and Thistlewood, who were the chief members of the revolutionary wing. Evans seems to have hoped much from their grand schemes, but to have taken care not to be involved in any of them—to the revolutionists' disgust. Like Wedderburn and Davenport, he preferred the pen to the sword.

Besides preaching, lecturing, and selling Spence's pamphlets, he wrote three tracts. The first of these, " Christian Policy the Salvation of the Empire," was published in 1816, and went through two editions. It was sold, price 1s. 6d., at Evans's shop, 8, Newcastle Street, Strand, and consists of an introduction, five pages, and forty-eight pages of closely printed matter. His pamphlet purports to be " a clear and concise examination into the causes that have produced the unavoidable National Bankruptcy and the effects that must ensue unless averted by the adaptation of this real and desirable remedy which would elevate these realms to a pitch of greatness hitherto unattained by any nation that ever existed."

England is on the verge of bankruptcy. She has lost her monopoly of the corn trade. Chaos will be caused by the failure of trade, and England will soon be in as bad a state as Ireland. The remedy is to levy taxes which people are too poor to pay. Hence capital must be taxed and paper money used. " The people are starving in the midst of that plenty their industry has produced." There are three ways of ending the misery. Two of them are : starve as Malthus suggests, steal and be hanged. Paper money does not produce trade, but trade makes paper a circulating medium. At present England has lost her liberty, she is under the Vienna Congress of Kings.

There have been three great eras in the world, that of Moses, of Christianity, of Alfred. Now a new one is at hand. From the time of Moses men have struggled against despots. The Jews were intended to have their own land, to sit under their own vine and fig-tree. The Church, i.e. Roman Catholic, Greek, and others emanating from them in the Christian epoch, is the " broadest Republic " known. Its ministers and officials are elected. All land and property belongs to the community, not to the individual. " The territory of a nation is the people's farm." But corruption and paganism have frustrated the intention of the Church. Christ tried to enforce obedience to the laws of Moses. The present enlightenment of Europe is due to Alfred's " Mosaic diffusion of the natural property of the nation among the people." America is the only country left that has a constitution, but America must beware. Patriots like the Sidneys, Russells, and Hampdens have tried to regain the liberties of the time of Alfred, but the land must first be restored.

" All the land, the waters, the mines, the houses, and all permanent feudal property must return to the people, the whole people, and be administered in partnership like that of the Church." The East India Company is an example of such a partnership. If the French Republic had established a partnership in land no imperial tyranny could have raised its head. The Norman Conquest destroyed the constitution of our pious ancestors. Evans has lived long enough to see the evils of heavy taxation. Liberty must be restored, and Malthus spurned. The debt must be cancelled. Sinking funds are no use. Trade alone will restore wealth.

Then he ushers in his remedy.

The land is the people's farm. There is to be no tenure but leasehold, no National Debt, no taxation, no alteration in the established form of government. All land, mines, etc., to be held in parochial or other "small partnerships." Each parish is to be the proprietor of a part of the national estate. A Board or Committee is to be appointed to lease or let the land. The King, the Lords, the Commons, the Clergy, the teachers in universities, colleges and schools, the judges in the courts, are all to be paid for their work.

"The great philosopher and law-giver Moses, as the projector of a system to put mankind in the possession of the land Nature intended for their use, is venerated as the Servant of God, but Joshua [*sic*] the Son of Joseph and Mary, who is said to have established this division of rents of the land (which the Church practises) . . . is esteemed a divinity!" The permanence of the Roman Catholic Church, in spite of its worldliness and idolatry, proves the advantage of the Plan. The Church only has its land, but England has her industries too. His scheme would give paper money real worth because it would increase trade. The results of Spenceanism would be :—

The nobility would be free to study and devote itself to legislation.

Religious intolerance would be destroyed.

Litigation would decrease.

There would be a proper system of representation and no corruption.

The right type of person for a representative would be produced.

The Debt would be liquidated.

The Government would be efficient and there would be no taxation.

The rich would be happy, the poor contented. Industry would be established, everyone would be his own master and interested in production.

It is easy to see from this summary that Evans could easily attract attention from those who were not able to criticize his knowledge or his reasoning. He is a religious man—though he has his own peculiar religion—and he has tried to show that a scriptural basis can be found for Spenceanism both in the Old and New Testament. Land is to be nationalized, and not only land, but water, mines, and " permanent feudal property "—whatever that may be. He sees that " parochial partnerships " may not always be possible, and suggests that there may be other groupings of partners. Probably he was thinking of industrial undertakings. He insists on the importance of commerce and industry and on the connection between depreciation of the paper-currency and trade depression. He realizes, too, that the revenue and expenditure of the country must be known before his Plan can be carried out. He contemplates no alteration in the system of Government or class-divisions. Present occupiers of land are not to be disturbed, while those individuals or associations who suffer in the transfer are to be indemnified or pensioned. The revolution is to be carried out by law ; public opinion will produce the law, and public opinion will be produced by self-interest.

It was a bright idea to select the Roman Catholic Church as a kind of Spencean Society, but the idea required more careful handling than he could give it. It would be only too easy to use it as an argument against Spenceanism.

His next tract was " Christian Policy in Full Practice Among the People of Harmony." It is unsigned, but it is so like Evans's other writings that it must surely be his. He wrote it after his release from prison in 1817, and it was published in 1818.[1] The description of Harmony is taken from Mellish's travels. This is followed by " Spence's Plan of Agrarian Fellowship." He calculates that out of £150,000,000 revenue there should be £75,000,000 balance when the King, the Lords, the Commons, the judges, the teachers, have been paid and the indemnities made over to those who require compensation. The King, by the way, is to have the same sum as that set apart for compensation, namely £20,000,000.

This tract is dated November 1818, and was " published by order of the Society of Christian Philanthropists. Sold by William Watling, 409, Strand, opposite the Adelphi, and at the Meeting House, every evening, No. 6, Archer Street, Golden Square, and by all vendors of tracts."

His last publication was " A Brief Sketch of the Life of Mr. Thomas Spence, Author of the Spencean

[1] H.O., 40. 7. " Jan. 27th, 1818 . . . Old Evans is preparing a book for publication. His former MS. was burnt by Carr, into whose hands he had entrusted it before his arrest."

System of Agrarian Fellowship or Partnership in Land, with an illustration of his Plan in the example of the village of Little Dalby, Leicestershire, accompanied with a selection of the songs sung in all the sections of the Spencean Society, by Thomas Evans, formerly Librarian to that Institution, Manchester, published by the Author, number 8 Short Street, Oldham Street, and sold by all Booksellers and Newsvendors." 1821.

Evans not only admired Spence, he was personally attached to him. He never criticizes his leader or pushes forward his own ideas. It is *Spence's* Plan that he is advertising. He was anxious that his friend's merits should be known to posterity. His references in his poems to " good Tommy Spence " are fraternal, and he carried his enthusiasm to such a pitch that he ends his " Life of Spence " with :—

" . . . Now if there has lived since the days of the Redeemer, one person more than another, that has imitated what is related of that great character in the Scriptures . . . it has been this friend of his species . . . the admirable Thomas Spence."

The revolutionaries hoped to compass their revolution with the aid of the reformers and disaffected in London. Preston accordingly invited Orator Hunt to organize a meeting at Spa Fields to consider parliamentary reform. The meeting was held on November 15, 1816. It was arranged to adjourn it until December 2nd, so that an answer might be given by the Regent to their petition. At the second of these meetings Thistlewood and the Watsons succeeded in causing a small riot. The riot, trifling and futile in itself, served the cause of Spence by giving it a grand advertisement, for the Government, anxious to prove that drastic measures were necessary if the growing disorder in the country was to be checked, made the most of the " Rebellion of the Six Men with their stockingful of ammunition."

There was much debating in Parliament over the political societies, and the Spencean Philanthropists were specially singled out for attention. An Act suppressing various societies received the Regent's signature on March 31, 1817, " and whereas certain societies or clubs calling themselves Spenceans, or Spencean Philanthropists hold and possess for their object the confiscation and division of the land, and the extinction of the funded property of the kingdom, and whereas it is expedient and necessary that all such societies and clubs as aforesaid should be utterly suppressed and prohibited as unlawful combinations and confederacies highly dangerous to the peace and tranquillity of this kingdom and to the constitution and government thereof as by law established, be it enacted that from and after the passing of this Act all societies and clubs calling themselves Spencean or Spencean Philanthropists and all the societies and clubs by whatever name or description the same are called or known who hold and profess the same objects and doctrines shall be and the same are utterly suppressed and prohibited as being unlawful combinations and conspiracies against the government of our sovereign Lord the King and against the peace and security of His Majesty's liege subjects." [1]

[1] See Hansard, 1817. Place quotes this Act, 27808, p. 230. 27 Geo. III., C. 19.

Not only were the rioters arrested, but many of the leading Spenceans. Evans's former misdemeanours had not been forgotten, and on the strength of his friendship with the Spa Field leaders he and his son, aged twenty, " a well-read studious youth, very modest in his demeanour and of good speech," were arrested on Sunday, February 9, 1817.[1]

They were both taken to the Home Office at Whitehall and put into a room with Watson, Preston, Keen, and Castle (the informer). Evans was examined by the Privy Council, and then sent to the House of Correction, Middlesex. He there, in presence of the King's Messenger, demanded a copy of the commitment. He had to share a room with a criminal who had turned King's evidence. Having drawn up a petition to the House of Commons, he despatched it thither, but learnt from his wife that it had gone to Whitehall. He had then to instruct his solicitor to gain possession of the petition or else to ask for permission to present another. After much delay on the part of the authorities the petition was presented to the House by the Hon. Henry Grey Bennett. Evans was examined six times. While these examinations were taking place the Habeas Corpus Act was suspended. He asked to be released on bail, but he and his son were sent to Horsemonger Lane, Surrey County Gaol. There they were separated and treated like felons. Evans was lodged in a " condemned " cell. He had only a bundle of rags for a bed, a pail for water, a chair and a trestle. He could have no candle. The fire was extinguished at dusk; while it

[1] Hone, *Reformists' Register*, August 1816.

was alight he had only a stick and piece of tin for poker and shovel. He had no box for his clothes. Instead of consoling himself with his flute, which was taken away from him, he had to listen to the condemned criminals immediately beneath him. On the third day his irons were removed. Three magistrates who paid a visit of inspection approved of these arrangements. Only his wife could visit him, and she had to talk through a grating in the presence of the turnkey. As a result of his complaints he was given a feather bed, his flute was returned, he was allowed to have candles, and to exercise himself in a passage. On July 27th he was removed to his son's room. His son had suffered similarly. No one but Mrs. Evans was allowed to see either of them.

According to Mrs. Evans, Sir Nathaniel Conant interviewed her husband and son on July 1st. He offered to release them in recognizances of £100 to appear before the Court of King's Bench when called upon to answer the charges against them. Both wanted to know what charges these were. Evans senior asked for the name of the person who had given information against him. But Sir Nathaniel Conant refused to give them any satisfaction, although it was he who had committed them. He then attempted to ignore the pair, but Evans turned on him and accused him of forging the commitment! Sir Nathaniel tried to interview Evans senior alone, but as he persisted in his assertions, the son was sent for and Sir Nathaniel tried to win him over in a separate interview, but without success. In fact, the police officer in the room had to interpose. In the middle of the storm Evans senior returned and proceeded to tell Sir Nathaniel what *he* thought of him.

" Take him away," said Sir Nathaniel.

" Who'll take him away ? " Evans exclaimed. However, his son led him off, and he went downstairs inveighing loudly against the proceedings. He met Lord Sidmouth on the stairs. Lord Sidmouth hastily withdrew !

Mrs. Evans, who had kept on the little shop during her husband's imprisonment, went to visit them on July 28th. Soon after her return home they appeared ! They had been discharged unconditionally and without any warning.

In the " Return of Persons Committed for Treason," 1817, which was printed, March 5, 1818, by order of the House of Commons, Thomas Evans, aged fifty-four, brace-maker, and Thomas J. Evans his son, are entered as imprisoned on suspicion of high treason.

The case of the two Evanses made a great stir. Reformers in Parliament, who were indignant at the state of the prisons and at the treatment of political offenders, made the most of the opportunity it afforded. Evans's petition was published in *The Times*, February 17, 1818, and Mrs. Evans's account of the interview with Sir N. Conant also appeared. *The Times* agreed with the *Independent Whig* that as the Evanses were imprisoned before the passing of the Suspension Act, they ought to have had a legal acquittal. Of course the Radicals took up the case. They sympathized with Evans as a martyr to Governmental tyranny. Sympathetic accounts of the

Spenceans and of their Plan appeared in Hone's "Broadsheets," in Cobbett's *Regiser* in the "Black Dwarf," the *Independent Whig*, and other Radical publications. Strangest of all, Southey, who took up the cudgels on behalf of the Government, found himself interested, not in Evans, but in Spence and Spenceanism. Meetings were held at the "Crown and Anchor" to raise subscriptions for the Evanses and other unfortunates. Place was specially invited by Galloway to attend the meeting on January 22, 1818, for the discussion of the measures to be taken. Notices of meetings and lists of subscribers were published in *The Times*, and at the meeting on February 3rd, when the subscription was opened, Evans and others were invited to address the meeting.[1]

The Government had played still further into the hands of the Spenceans by trying to secure a conviction for high treason against the conspirators instead of for incitement to riot. This together with the treatment of the Evanses and the exposure of Castle, a Spencean who had doubled the parts of chief conspirator and spy, metamorphosed the rioters into popular heroes.

The Spenceans evidently profited from this publicity. They continued to hold meetings and, to judge from the nervous watchfulness of the Government, their Society seems to have been popular in their own circles. Evans and his friends were certainly very active. It must have been this popularity that encouraged Evans to publish the tract "Christian Policy in Full Practice . . ." in 1818. He had not

[1] See Place, Journals, 39, p. 251, etc.

dared to publish it before. He continued to be friendly with revolutionists, but his fellows kept aloof.

The Festal Day of the Society was Thomas Spence's birthday, which was celebrated with feast and song. On July 2, 1817, a supper was given at the " Cock " in remembrance of him. Evans's " The Memory of Spence " must have been composed for one of these occasions. " Should Thomas Spence e'er be forgot." (Tune : " Old Lang Syne ".)

> His books and songs for forty years
> He's published many ways.
> For which he oft was sent to Jail
> Grant him your meed of praise.
> And never let him be forgot
>   Though he is gone from hence.

The last celebration took place at the Navy Coffee House, Catherine Street, Strand, in 1819, when Davenport recited his elegy on Spence.

> Lycurgus, Minos, Numa, Solon, all
> The Stars of Ancient Greece and Rome may fall
> But thy pale light shall in its orbit run
> Bright and as changeless as the glorious Sun
> And shine through every age, in every clime,
> While Nature's pulse beats to the ma;ch of time.
>
> That man, that honest man was Thomas Spence,
> Whose genius, judgment, wit and manly sense
> Confounded all the dogmas of the schools
> And proved that Statesmen are but learned fools,
> That priests preach future worlds of pain and bliss
> To cheat the weak and rob the poor in this,
> Or else their practice and their cry would be,
> Let all be equal and let all be free !

It was the activities of Thistlewood that brought the Society to an end. Between the two Spa Field meetings and from the time of the meetings until the final catastrophe in 1820,[1] Thistlewood, Preston, and their friends were all mystery and dark intrigue. The proposals of the Spenceans to confiscate landed property, the revolutionary talk of the " conspirators," the constant meetings of both sets kept the Government on the alert, and the daily doings of the Spenceans were carefully recorded by spies, one or two of whom were, professedly, Spenceans themselves. Evidently, even social gatherings had to be abandoned, to avert suspicion of complicity with Thistlewood and his companions.

[1] I.e. the Cato Street Conspiracy.

CHAPTER VIII

THE THOUGHT OF SPENCE

It is time now to examine Spence's thought more closely.

He proposes to nationalize the land which is to be administered for the nation by the parish councils, who are to be controlled by the central government. His Plan will entail a reform of the local and central governing bodies. Both are to be representative, the franchise is to be extended and voting by ballot introduced. Certain other reforms, such as the establishment of universal military training, are to be carried out. By thus nationalizing the land he hoped to secure to every man his means of subsistence. If this were done, he was convinced that all the evils of society would be cured.

Unfortunately, in spite of his many tracts, his debates and arguments, and his tireless efforts to explain and convert, Spence never succeeded in making his Plan clear. He failed also to answer some serious criticisms of his scheme.

In the first place, Spence thinks in terms of land. This is due, probably, to the influence of Harrington and the Physiocrats. England, of course, was far more rural than she is now, but it is strange that a man who never lived in the country, who spent all his life in Newcastle and in London, should not have considered what modifications of his scheme might be necessary if towns and industrial undertakings were to be fitted into it. His description of the capital of Crusonia, and of the state of trade both in that country and in Spensonia, shows that modern conditions were not wholly absent from his thought. The parishes are to control the mines and fisheries. Those parishes which have no land, presumably town parishes, are to remain without any. Spence's dream was of a Utopia where commerce and industry should subordinate themselves to agriculture. It is to be remarked that his chief consideration to trade is given in " Crusonia," 1782, and in his publications 1798–1814. External events, commercial developments in Newcastle, controversies over the state of the market, unemployment, bullion, in London during the period 1798–1814, may account for this consideration. Or friends may have drawn his attention to the matter. Evans's influence was manifesting itself after 1798. The fact remains, however, that Spence has not really worked out his scheme in its application to commerce, industry, and town parishes. It was during the years 1792–98 that Spence was trying to make his Plan known in London. It was unfortunate that just then his Plan should have been most rural.

He bases his Plan on the fact that private ownership of land is unjustifiable. His account of the origin of private property is absurd, though perhaps not more absurd than that of other contemporary thinkers.

How, for instance, does he know that usurpers of land—the ancestors of many owners—were never called to account, or indeed that they were usurpers?

Nevertheless, though he fails in the attempt to prove private ownership unjustifiable by disclosing how private property originated, he does give a graphic description of the chief evils likely to arise from private ownership, and thus he shows that it is undesirable.

But the great difficulty is that though Spence meant the land to be nationalized and administered by parish councils under the control of a central government, his intention has to be deduced from what he says. It is nowhere definitely stated. Indeed, certain of his remarks might lead one to a very different conclusion.

From a cursory reading of his tracts it would appear that Spence simply intended to parcel out the land among the various parishes, and that the members of each parish were to form themselves into a corporation which was to have the same power over its territory as a lord of the manor over his land and houses, and was to be " sovereign lord of its own territories." This corporation was to administer the land for its own benefit and share out the profits among the members.

If his intention was merely to substitute a corporation for the individual landlord, he would be conferring a questionable benefit upon mankind, as modern experience of trusts, companies, and even town corporations, could be made to show. The force of public opinion may be sufficient to make great public bodies such as the L.C.C. act for the public good, but there are innumerable instances of small town and rural councils whose actions are directed by private rather than public interests. The servant of a corporation is necessarily very much at its mercy, and his possession of a share or a vote is not always an adequate safeguard. Spence does not make clear what is to compel the corporation to expend its profits on local improvements. Instances come readily to the mind of councils whose policy in regard to the expenditure of the ratepayers' money has been dictated by local jealousies, by the private interest of the councillors, or by too great a desire to save the rate-payers' pockets. Under Spence's system this might lead to the parish corporation having too great an eagerness for large dividends, or for purely commercial and industrial undertakings.

Some of the corporations would be enormously wealthy. The few actual residents in the business quarters of great cities like London, caretakers, watchmen, and one or two clergymen, would be very rich men, but mankind would not benefit ! If coal were discovered in a parish, the corporation would simply lease out the mining rights for as high a rental as it could procure and live on the rent and royalties it drew. The corporations would in fact be exactly like commercial companies owning lands and interested in industrial undertakings.

How did Spence propose to check a rush from the poor parishes to the wealthy ones ? Perhaps he imagined a kind of levelling process taking place when the system was inaugurated. Immigration might

bring the wealth of the richer ones to the level of
the poorer ones.   But there is another consideration.
The corporations would not want strangers in their
parishes unless their presence was a source of profit,
unless, for example, they were skilled workers necessary
for the development of local industries.   The History
of the English Poor Law would furnish illustrations
of this difficulty ; the attitude of some modern
authorities towards strangers likely to complicate the
housing problem might be adduced or the determination of some progressive local authorities to keep
positions and prizes away from alien applicants.   In
fact, Spence's corporations would tend to become close,
and strangers would not readily gain admission to
them.

Spence proposes to abolish taxation. " There are
no tolls or taxes of any kind . . . but the aforesaid
rent."   But he does not really do so.   Rates and
taxes are simply added on to the rent.   The individual
pays a lump sum comprising rent, rates, and taxes,
and the directors of the corporation transmit a lump
sum to the Government as the corporation's share of
the taxation.

It is not easy to see why rents should be lower or
less of a burden.   The proposed saving effected by
collecting the taxes in this way would be a drop in
the ocean, if, indeed, there were any at all.   If the
men in the parish consented to giving the women and
children each a dividend, it might only be because
such an arrangement would entitle the men, as trustees
for their wives, children, and sisters, to have larger
dividends.   There is nothing to guarantee that the

women would have control over their shares or that the children would actually benefit. True, Spence advocates universal suffrage, and there is to be a central Parliament, but the representatives of his parish groups would simply be delegates of the property-owning corporations.

Most of these objections were put to Spence by his critics. The latter were inclined to take him too literally, and Spence, of course, was unconscious of the fact that he had only partly explained what he meant. Thus neither the critics nor Spence arrived at the crux of the matter.

Spence's adversary in the " Interesting Conversation " contends that corporation government is not always successful. People in general would reap little benefit from their landed property. " There is too much party work." Spence answers this by pointing out the necessity of reforming the system of local government. He forgets that he has been talking of the corporations as though they owned the parish land—a very different matter from administering it. He complains in the " End of Oppression " that enemies of the Spencean system say that the parish would mismanage its funds. He thinks that if state funds can be managed, then so can parish funds. Unfortunately, he does not ask himself why the state is fairly honest financially. Instead, he resorts to sarcasm. Why should Plebeians, he asks in his " Recantation of the 'End of Oppression '," be troubled with rents and landed property when they are accustomed to neither ? If a gentleman left a benefit society an estate, of course it would not know how to deal with it.   Only the rich are sober, industrious, and honest.

He implies everywhere that corporation government is the only solution of the difficulty, for, as he explains, private ownership is not to be tolerated, and an equal division of landed property is impracticable.   He has one quaint reason for thinking that a number of people acting in the capacity of landlord would be better than one.   There would be more heads to think out improvements.

He thought that the danger of having too wealthy or too poor parishes would be overcome by the Government's preventing the wealthy parishes from being selfish or jealous of strangers and foreigners, while the poorer parishes could be allowed to send the wealthy ones their surplus poor.

He tried to answer criticisms based on financial considerations by practical illustrations.   He imagines the scheme being carried out in the parish of Little Dalby, Leicestershire, and he selects for his purpose certain details given in Nicholl's " History of Leicestershire " for the year 1776.   These are : number of houses, 21 ; families, 22 ; population, 123 ; wages, winter 1s., summer 1s. 3d., harvest 1s. 6d. per day ; cost of the poor for 1776, £27 16s. ; rents, £1,422 5s. per annum.   To this £1,422 5s. Spence adds £100 as the rent of the ex-landlord's own land.

He draws up the following budget :—

	£	s.	d.
Total rents..	1,522	5	0
Sum to be paid in taxes at 4s. in the £ ($\frac{1}{5}$ × £1,522 5s.)	304	9	0
∴ Sum to be divided among the 123 inhabitants	1,217	16	0
Individual share (about)	9	18	0

This £304 9s. is to include local as well as national expenses !

But who forms Spence's parish corporation ? From 1796 Spence would have answered : All the 123 inhabitants, men, women, and children. The children could only form part of the corporation in the sense that their shares were allotted to them. Were their shares to be reserved for them until they were of age, or were their fathers to dispose of the amounts for them ? Spence does not settle these points, though he implies that the shares are to be paid to the children each year. Really, all the dividend scheme amounts to is a yearly rebate on rent. It put a premium upon large families and a tax upon single people and childless married couples, though these could turn the tax into a premium by sharing houses, i.e. if there were any surplus. A man who received a rebate of £10 on a £20 a year rent might naturally ask to pay only £10 in future. Spence would have argued that the following year local and governmental expenditure might reduce or increase the rebate. In practice people would come to pay—as before—the rent plus the amount deemed necessary for rates and taxes and no more.

It was pointed out to Spence that even if the dividend worked out at £10 in Little Dalby, the larger population of other parishes would not permit of such a dividend, that the expenditure of the state would be heavy, and that local expenditure would much reduce the dividend. His reply was to the effect that public control of public expenses would make for economy, and that there might be mines to develop.[1]

[1] Vide " Perfect Commonwealth," VII and VIII.

He takes for granted that the discovery of coal in a parish would make no difference to the working out of his Plan.

The dividend part of the Plan is not vital to it, but here, as elsewhere, Spence's general principles must be sought. He is anxious that the administration shall be carried out as economically as possible, that the system of taxation shall be simple, and that the taxpayer shall have a minimum of payments to make. This could be best effected if payments to the state were made by the local councils and not by the individual. Again, he wants to ensure that the actual members of the parishes shall benefit from their own thrift and zeal.

If Spence meant England to be divided into a number of small republics, each owning territory about the size of a parish, and each sending delegates to a vaguely delineated central government, which could have no real control of these republics, as each *owned* its territory, then his scheme is absurd, and any one of the objections raised would do to prove its absurdity. The most obvious is one given in the Preface to the " Restorer," that his scheme would lead to endless feuds and civil wars, especially as each parish has a bit of an army.

But if the land were to be nationalized, and if the local governments were simply to be administrators holding all their authority from a central government which represented the nation, then his Plan is both intelligible and practicable. Indeed, during the last century or so, his Plan seems in process of piecemeal and haphazard realization.

Both Southey and Place construe Spence as meaning this, and his disciple, Thomas Evans, says definitely that the land is the people's farm and is to be nationalized. Evans actually thinks of England as an industrial and commercial country, and suggests that the Church might lead the way and begin to work out the Plan on its lands. Davenport, who follows Evans, would begin with a single college and farm run on Spencean lines. Like Evans, he thinks that the Church might lead the way.

Are these interpreters of his thought correct? It can be shown from what Spence himself says and implies that they are.

There can be no doubt that Spence was thinking of his parish governments as administrators rather than as owners of the parish property, and that he was thinking of political sovereignty as residing in the central government, although he apparently regards ownership of the land as conferring political sovereignty.

In " Crusonia " parish affairs are to be determined by the majority, and each parish is to have all the " uncontrollable power that can possibly be made good use of by a corporation and be connected only by a Parliament for the common strength and welfare of the whole." The parishes are to be independent states of so small a size that a central government is possible. This central government is to " hinder them from altering their own constitutions," to be a defence against the injustices of one Crusonian state to another, and to prevent foreign states hostile to Crusonia injuring her. The central government is to control the state militias through the general it appoints and to conduct foreign policy. He states clearly what the duties of the parish government are to be and describes the central Parliament.

At this point a difficulty arises. " Crusonia " is a supplement to the Lecture, and the first edition of the Lecture is missing. One cannot, therefore, compare the Plan that Spence divulged to his Newcastle readers with that given to his London readers. The 1793 edition of the Lecture cannot be used here in the place of the 1775 edition, for this reason. Between them the two " Spensonias " reproduce " Crusonia " with some important omissions. Neither version describes the system of government under the new scheme so clearly. The duties of the local governments and the relation of the central to the local government are not defined as exactly.

Did Spence make these omissions because he felt that his meaning was plain enough without them, or did he think that the relationship of the central and local government was an insignificant part of the scheme ?

Perhaps the truth is that the Newcastle Plan was better worked out. Spence conceived it and fashioned it when a young man of twenty-five to thirty-two. He was weary and embittered before he began to advertise it in London. His Plan was so firmly fixed in his own mind that in his anxiety to stress its less ordinary parts and to add improvements he would leave his reader to understand his meaning by implication rather than definition.

It is best, therefore, to confirm the interpretation

of his Plan by means of the London publications, 1793–1814, and to regard " Crusonia " as corroboratory evidence.

First, who did really own the land, according to Spence ? He is always insisting that the earth belongs to mankind in common, and that the " land or earth in any country or neighbourhood . . . belongs at all times to the living inhabitants of the said country or neighbourhood in an equal manner." Before his system is established " the whole people in some country " are to agree that " every man has an equal property in the land in the neighbourhood where he resides." The corporation is not to alienate its lands.

He actually says : " Let every parish form itself into a corporation and take possession of the land in its own neighbourhood." What he thought was : Let the people in each parish meet together and say that the land is not to belong to private individuals, but each individual is to assert his right to a share of it, i.e. it is nationalized piecemeal. The land is to be treated as public property, and so, of course, the rents will be public property. The rest of the Plan is the method by which the public property will be administered. He sees the " Parish Republics " as " benefit or fraternal societies," i.e. they are political bodies discharging certain economic or social functions.

Many passages from his other publications might be cited to substantiate what has been said. His dislike of private ownership is continually being emphasized. He says in " Spensonia " : " Private property in land is unjust according to the law of Nature. If the people wish to have the Government in their own hands . . . they must begin first by taking the land under their own hands." The Spensonians " declared the property of the island to be the property of them all collectively," though the members of each parish were responsible for the territory allotted to them.

God alone is Lord of the Universe, " Mankind in their respective districts are His substitutes and deputies."

It is disconcerting, however, to find Spence declaring positively that he does not believe in land nationalization. " I would not have the land national nor provincial but parochial property." [1] His explanation " that the people might be as much interested as possible both in the improvement of their estates " and in the spending of public money shows that his mind was occupied with the question of administration, not of ownership. The rest of the passage is also elucidatory. He talks of the Government as something quite detached from the people, and of land-nationalizing as causing all the profit to go to the Government to be spent on foreign conquest. He is falling into the error of identifying the abstract term " government " with the concrete image of His Majesty King George III's Ministers. He evidently thought that these Ministers would pocket the profits.

His anxiety to have a proper system of local government with the parish councils as the effective units, and a central government which shall give the parish councils full play and not arrogate to itself undue power, has led him to stress the part played by the parish council and to give insufficient consideration to the central government.

[1] " Restorer," p. 36. (" Important Trial," 1803.)

Nevertheless, Spence is thinking of his parish republics as parts of a national state, bound together in a federal union by a central government to which they owe obedience.

It is the whole people in some country who are to declare the land theirs. Spensonia is thought of as a country inhabited by a nation state. It has a written constitution. The constitutions he draws up are for nation-states. Sovereignty is declared to reside in the people, though actually it resides in the central government.

Even in his lectures it is clear that the central government has the political sovereignty which ultimately resides in the nation, because universal suffrage is established. The whole people are to make the change and to agree to the fundamentals of the new constitution. The central government is evidently the legislature, for it allows the parishes the power of putting the laws in force in all cases. It also levies taxes.

The central government is obviously meant to prevent the parishes quarrelling with one another or alienating their lands and is to compel them to look after their own poor, build houses, and let the land publicly to the best bidder.

Strangers and foreigners who needed poor relief were to be maintained by the state. The generals for the militia were provided by the state. The legislature was to see that wealthy parishes did not make selfish regulations. The surplus poor in the more burdened parishes were to be distributed amongst the wealthier parishes. The latter proposition would only be feasible if the central government were to regulate the matter. Not only is the central government to keep peace amongst the parishes, but there will be national courts to administer justice.

When Spence is thinking of the " public " good, he is not necessarily thinking parochially, he is thinking of the " whole people." Parliament (i.e. the central government) is to purchase secrets from inventors and publish them for the sake of public utility.

This interpretation of his Plan, then, may be accepted, though it does not explain all Spence's confusions and inconsistencies. His misrepresentation of his own thought was bound to lead him into contradictions. Enough has been said to indicate what these were, but one or two further instances may be given.

Spence tackled the wealthy parish difficulty not only by referring to the central government but by imagining an influx of people pouring into Spensonia. People would be drawn thither by the desire of benefiting from the Plan. If some parishes suffered from a rush of people no harm would be done, because the competition for houses would increase rents, and so the dividends would be higher. He ignores the fact that even if the dividends are higher there will be more people to receive them. Besides, according to his view, Spensonia in its relation to the world is in the position of a rich parish to a host of poorer ones. How will he check the rush to Spensonia ?

He would dispose easily of the landlords, their servants, and all who would lose their positions if his regime were established immediately.

Landlords and lawyers (the landlords' allies) would be free to trade and farm. They would only be deprived of their landed property, so that their goods and chattels would make them much better off than everyone else. Soldiers and sailors could be sent to their own parishes, pensioned, and employed to train others. As to the remaining officials, they would have to trust to the tenderness of their fellow parishioners! Spence does not consider cost!

In drawing up constitutions for his Spensonia, he was aiming at greater definiteness and exactitude.

At first reading, it seems as though Spence were bound to dispel his worst ambiguities. Unfortunately, instead of avoiding confusion, he has run straight into it, for the simple reason that he has tried to adapt to his scheme a French Constitution, which he does not understand. He apparently thought of the Legislative Body and Executive Council described in the French Constitution as a kind of English Parliament, and of the primary and electoral assemblies as corresponding to parochial and county councils. One instance of the resulting confusion must suffice. Spence has, for the most part, just substituted " parochial " for " primary " in the constitution that he used, and has inserted a few clauses summarizing the Plan. Consequently he gives his " primary assembly " administrative functions which the French Constitution expressly declares that it is not to have.

When the worst is said, though, Spence's Plan can be understood in spite of its obscurities. Naturally he himself was sure that it was plain enough for the meanest intelligence, as is evident in his letter to Charles Hall in June 1807.

" I am sorry that we cannot better agree. And I am sorry not only on my own account but on account of the Poor whom we both mean to serve. For I do not think writers will be able to benefit mankind much in a political way until they unanimously conclude on some effectual Plan for the Purpose. . . . If I could not point out plainly and palpably to them [men] a Land flowing with Milk and Honey . . . I would leave them quietly in their bondage. . . . It would be ridiculous as well as criminal in me, Sir, to show modesty and pretend that I do not know my own Plan and the full tendency of it. For I do. . . . I hope that you will excuse me for being thus frank when you consider that I am compelled to be so in Justice to Myself, my Fellow-Creatures and to You. . . ."

CHAPTER IX

SPENCEANISM AND MODERN SOCIALISM

Has Spence made any contribution to the world of thought ? The idea that a man's subsistence should be secured to him is old, and so, too, is the idea that the actual territory of a nation, tribe, family, or town, does not ultimately belong to the private individual. But when Spence gave them utterance they had the force of new ideas and were capable of initiating important developments.

To some extent Spence was thinking along the same lines as contemporary writers who also wanted to make each man certain of some means of subsistence or to mitigate the evils arising from too great inequalities of wealth. But Spence's line of thought is distinct from any of these. Godwin's economic arrangements were to suit a world made perfect. Thomas Paine, writing at a time when Spence's Plan must have become well known to dwellers in the metropolis, wants to establish a national fund so that everyone at the age of twenty-one may receive the " sum of fifteen pounds sterling, to enable him or her to begin the world ; and also ten pounds sterling per annum during life to every person now living of the age of fifty years," and to all others when they attain the age of fifty. The lame and blind are also to have an annuity of £10. Paine regards the earth as belonging to mankind in common, and one-tenth of the capital of the country is, he considers, equivalent in value to the value of the original estate of mankind, now absorbed in the possession of others. This one-tenth is to provide the fund.

Ogilvie had published an essay in 1781. He advocates a new land system which will obviate the necessity of Poor Laws and diminish the temptation to crime. He aimed at the establishment of peasant proprietorships which would result in an equal division of property among men. He vested the ultimate ownership of the land in the " lords of the manor," and every man who acquired an allotment (assigned to him in perpetuity provided he paid the rent due) was to pay " certain aid and services of a feudal nature to the Lord of the Manor."

Charles Hall, writing more than ten years after Spence published his lecture in London, inveighs against private ownership of land and wants wealth to be equally divided.

These brief résumés are enough to show that Spence's remedies had nothing in common with them. He is continually expressing his disapproval of schemes for equalizing wealth in his publications and in his private letters.

He criticizes Paine's scheme on the ground that it will turn the poor into paupers dependent on the charity of the nation. He asks why only one-tenth is to be claimed by the people. As to a scheme of a " feudal nature," the idea would have been anathema to Spence, though he was interested in Ogilvie's essay.

No, he aimed at a system of public ownership of national wealth, which would secure to the nation the advantages of private ownership.

Hence, he insists on the leasing out of land on a lease long enough to benefit the individual and in small enough allotments to give the poor but thrifty farmer a fair chance. Hence, too, he insists on his parochial form of administration, on representative government in the parish as in the country, and on universal manhood suffrage.

Spence realized that the Government must abandon its *laissez-faire* policy, and realized, too, that this could be done without impeding the free play of industry and commerce.

The nineteenth century has seen the abandonment of the *laissez-faire* policy, at least as regards the health, personal security, and education of the worker. Spence discerned and pointed out this inevitable drift of national policy. He is, too, the forerunner of the groups of thinkers who since his day have advocated nationalization schemes.

He was continually crying out against all kinds of abuses, against exorbitant rents, the conduct of commercially minded landlords, sinecures, Government spies, and the press-gang. Short but pregnant tracts might be compiled from his writings entitled " Housing Reform," " Case again Communism and Equal Division of Property," " Poor Law," " Universal Suffrage," " Votes for Women," " Local Government," " Small Holdings," " Universal Military Training," " Single

Tax." Many of his proposals were then the common topics of reformers, but his pungency gives them freshness.

He wants the parish councils to be responsible for the housing of their districts. They should see that cottages are built properly, and they should undertake the repairs. They must not only see that there are sufficient cottages, but that there are apartments for those who do not require a whole house. The parishes were to be responsible for education, public libraries, and for the poor (with some state aid). Hospitals were to be maintained by the counties. His pictures of Crusonia and Spensonia, with their beautiful towns and houses, their fruit-trees, hedges, and their gardens, show him to be a forerunner of the Garden City founders.

He was anxious that women should share equally with men in the privileges as well as the duties of citizenship. They were to have the vote.

He anticipates also the views of some modern imperialists. He wanted Spensonia to have colonies so that it could help them to establish the Spensonian Constitution. Then he would declare them independent, and, assuming that they would ardently desire it, he would admit them into intimate friendship and alliance with the Mother Country.

If not wholly original, these views of Spence on the minor questions of his day were sufficiently uncommon to allow them to rank as small contributions to the world of thought.

It is not out of place here to notice how full his writings are of love for his fellow-creatures, how tender he is and how chivalrous. Women are to be equal with men, politically and economically, but their delicacy is to be spared. They are to vote, but not to undertake the arduous duties involved in holding official positions. He would like divorce made easier because it would make men more willing to forgive erring women. He cannot see why the illegitimate child should be distinguished from its fellows. He would make every fifth day a sabbath of rest.

But Spence is not just an isolated thinker whose thought is only resuscitated occasionally for the edification of the intellectually curious. It is possible to show that his ideas were broadcast through his own and his disciples' efforts, and also to link them with those of later thinkers.

Spenceanism was given prominence by Parliament and the Press in 1801 and in 1817. A study of the Parliamentary debates in 1817 [1] shows that the Government really had some fear of its influence. Parliament was not wildly excited,[2] but both the Government in its fear and the Opposition in its

---

[1] See Hansard.
[2] The voting on the Bills was as follows :—

SUSPENSION BILL.

House of Lords	..	2nd Reading	{ Content	84	Proxy 66
			Non-content 23		Proxy 35
House of Commons		1st Reading	Yeas	273	Noes 98
,, ,, ,,		3rd Reading	Yeas	265	Noes 103

SEDITIOUS MEETINGS BILL.

House of Lords	..	3rd Reading	{ Content	111	
			Non-content 23		
House of Commons		1st Reading	Ayes	190	Noes 14
,, ,, ,,		3rd Reading	Ayes	179	Noes 44

(*Annual Register*, 1817, pp. 20–33.)

disdain seem to show a lurking uneasiness at the threatened attack on property. Lord Liverpool said that there were two engines of conspiracy at work, one of which, the Spenceans, was "calculated to produce a complete convulsion in the elements which composed the system of social life." Let people only read the Spencean publications and they would realize the danger.

Lord Castlereagh " could produce the creed of the Society, not written in the style of low-bred mischief-makers, but with an elegance that would astonish the House."

Mr. Robinson declared that the Spenceans could be numbered in thousands.

By 1817 Spencean doctrines had become familiar to a sprinkling of members in both Houses of Parliament.

Then, as has been seen, the *Quarterly*, and the *Edinburgh Review* in its answer to the *Quarterly*, helped to advertise the Plan, and the Radical Press gave it a further advertisement.

By turning from debates and newspapers to the reports of the Secret Committee and to the Home Office Papers upon which the reports are based, it would seem possible to verify the statements of the Government as to Spenceanism being widespread in the country and the metropolis,[1] and so to trace currents of Spenceanism. But the exaggeration, due to alarm, has led those who supplied information and those who drew up the Report into inaccuracies and

[1] The Report says : " Your Committee find . . . that the doctrines of the Spencean clubs have been widely diffused through the country either by the extension of similar societies or by missionaries."

misrepresentations that obscure the truth. Reputable societies whose object was to agitate for parliamentary reform have been confounded with the wilder revolutionary societies.

Hampden Clubs or Union Societies were established in all the big towns and in many country villages. They were regarded with the same apprehension as the earlier Corresponding Society. As most of the clubs demanded Universal Suffrage and Annual Parliaments, the Government and many of its Whig opponents justly regarded them as revolutionary. At almost every political meeting where feeling ran high, and where the majority of those assembled were poor men, there was sure to be menacing talk of landholders and fundholders, confiscation of estates, and division of property. Suspicious and over-anxious magistrates, in fear of machine-smashing and rickburning, would be only too ready to make the most of such talk. The Manchester magistrates were notoriously alert. Zeal was quickened, too, by the rewards for information that loyal citizens might expect. If such talk did occur, the Government branded the society "Spencean," as nowadays it would be branded "Bolshevik." Such talk was "dangerous," and no attempt was made to prove that the society really was "Spencean." [1] Lord Cochrane said that Spencean principles were supposed to be prevalent in Glasgow, but that the name was unknown until it appeared in the newspapers.

[1] There must have been little to distinguish the wilder members of the Hampden Clubs from the wilder members of the Spencean Society.

The statement that Spenceanism was widespread in the metropolis and the country must not, therefore, be taken too literally. Nothing, for instance, can be learnt from letters warning the Government of dreadful conspiracies, of the Manchester mob's talk of the " row " it anticipated and the division of property it expected, of the purchase of guns in the Midlands, except, indeed, that the times were ripe for the propagation of Spenceanism. The unrest and the fears of the Government led to wild rumours. In the north of England report had it that the Bank was taken. In London the papers made much of a Chester meeting which proved to be a hoax.

The magistrates complain in their letters of the influence of Radical publications.[1] At Norwich, a Brunswick Club had been founded to oppose the Hampden Club, which it regarded as traitorous and revolutionary. It published a broadsheet deprecating the levelling principles of the Hampden Club and reproving the members for deserting their allies at Spa Fields on December 2nd. Evidently talk at the Norwich Hampden Club savoured of Spenceanism. Perhaps a detailed study of these societies at Norwich might reveal a current of Spenceanism that could be followed up.

On December 21, 1816, Mr. Lee Keck wrote to Lord Sidmouth from Stoughton Grange. He said that the clubs in his district made parliamentary reform their ostensible object, but openly regarded it as an introduction to Spence's Plan. He said that Preston talked of his directions issued to 15,000.

[1] H.O. Papers, 3. 4. 5.

He might have known better than to concern himself with Preston's remarks ! [1]

The clearest case is that of a letter from Mr. Baker, a Bath magistrate, to Lord Sidmouth in 1817.[2] He has interviewed Hickman, one of the leaders of the Bath Hampden Club, called the Union Society. Hickman was leaving the club because it had entered on the Spencean system.

In September 1817 R. Eaton, the keeper of the gaol at Derby, wrote in December to say that when he was escorting the convict Thomas Bacon to Sheerness, the latter told him that Grovenor Henson (a prisoner detained under the Suspension Act) had a plan to seize all the principal estates.[3]

The Police Reports,[4] in the Home Office Papers, establish a connection between Manchester and London. The London leaders of prominent societies were generally in touch with kindred societies in the big towns. Watson, Thistlewood, and Preston, the leaders of the Spenceans, were well known.

A Home Office letter, July 28, 1818, to Sir John Byng, comments on the quietness of Manchester, but asks him to look out for a man named Longbottom (probably an assumed name), as traces of a correspondence between him and the Spa Field gang had been detected. He was supposed to have influence over the out-of-work spinners. The Post Office was instructed to detain Longbottom's letters from Manchester. Another letter from Hobhouse to Byng talks of the general insurrection that was brewing.

[1] H.O., 40. 3.   [2] H.O., 40. 6.
[3] H.O., 40. 7.   Moggridge said that he knew Bacon (H.O., 40. 5).
[4] H.O., 79, 1–3.

Manchester was waiting for London to lead the way. Hunt and Thistlewood were in communication.

When Bamford was in London, 1817, he was introduced to the leading Spenceans. He saw the two Evanses in Cold Bath Fields Prison, and became acquainted with Thistlewood, Watson, and Alexander Galloway. He received his relief funds from Galloway, and, a few years later, when he was again in trouble, from the younger Evans.[1] In January 1818 Sir Nathaniel Conant, the magistrate, noted that four of the men from Manchester, who went to Westminster Hall to get their recognizances discharged, went to Evans's house in Newcastle Street and stayed there a considerable time.

Wooler and Pearson, the attorney, were with the men in court.

In 1820 T. J. Evans, old Evans's son, became editor of the *Manchester Observer*, a popular newspaper of great influence. He dared not advocate Spenceanism in his paper, but he was an ardent reformer. He announced in his first editorial that he intended to advocate Annual Parliaments, Universal Suffrage, and the Ballot. He wanted to bring Manchester into closer touch with London. He busied himself with collecting and distributing funds for the relief of prisoners. When invited to conduct a meeting of mechanics and artisans who wanted to present an address to the Queen, he wrote to them to explain how much he sympathized with them. He published a full account of the Cato Street Conspiracy, and admitted that he and his father had once been friends with Thistlewood. He reserved a corner of the paper

[1] Bamford, " Life of a Radical," ii.

for reviews of pamphlets and articles on reform and on political economy. He sold cheap pamphlets. It is highly probable that his father's Spencean " Works " were amongst these. Evans senior settled in Manchester, and it was there that he published his " Life of Spence " in 1821.

The settlement of the two Evanses in Manchester would seem to ensure their principles finding a home there also.

Unfortunately, T. J. Evans's career as an editor was cut short by his indictment for libel. He had freely criticized the military for the outrages in which the soldiers were concerned at Oldham, and had published a letter of his own criticizing the conduct of the Rev. W. R. Hay, whose arbitrary actions as a magistrate had aroused his indignation. Wooler took over the paper at the end of the year. On January 27, 1821, there was a paragraph on the Duke of Wellington's aristocratic opinions—his disdain of the mob and his view that property was the base of right. He is warned to be careful lest each member of the mob claims his share. In itself the paragraph is trivial, but in relation to the events of the period it is indicative of Spencean sympathies.

Thomas Preston, the lame shoemaker of Spa Field fame, was, like Evans, imbued with missionary zeal. It led him not only from public-house to public-house, and from one group of needy or unemployed workers to another, but also from London to Birmingham.[1]

[1] H.O., 40. 3. Preston brought Evans's book, " Spence's Plan," to the " Red Hart," Shoe Lane. If he found men there who were out of work, he would give them bread, beer, and cheese, saying that it was his duty to divide all equally.

He set out on November 22, 1817. His efforts were
not very successful, as the police were too vigilant.
Besides, he was too violent. He talked like a madman and drank too much. The police failed to trace
all his movements, but he probably visited other
places in addition to Birmingham. Report said that
he had gone to Lancashire, but as he returned from
Birmingham itself on November 28th, and was very
short of money, it is not probable.[1]

Spenceanism had spread then to areas outside the
metropolis, and Spencean ideas were familar to Radicals
and reformers in the provinces.

It is Robert Owen who is the connecting link between
Spence and later thinkers.

A study of Spenceanism and Owenism suggests that
Owen was developing the doctrines of Spence. It can
be shown that the thought of the two men is logically
connected, and that Owen had made the thought of
Spence part of his own gospel.

It will be remarked that it is not until 1814 that
the trend of Robert Owen's thought becomes definitely
economic. He had long looked upon himself as the
moral regenerator of society, but his philanthropy had
engaged itself in schemes for the social regeneration
and better education of his fellows.

The diversion of his thought was due to two causes,
the economic distress of the period 1812-20 and his
friendship with the economists of the period, notably
Ricardo, Malthus, and Place, with whom he became
familiar after 1812—from that year he was almost
continuously in London.

[1] H.O., 79. 3, and H.O., 40. 7. 134.

It is remarkable that as soon as Owen began to think in terms of economics, he began to develop views like Spence. A study of his publications from 1812–20 shows this economic development and this similarity to Spenceanism.

Briefly, Owen came to the conclusion that a solution of the unemployment problem was a necessary preliminary to the salvation of society.

His early publications give no hint of this economic trend. Podmore points out that his fourth essay in 1814 is a very different document from the previous ones, " there is a comprehensive and clearly reasoned scheme of Social Reconstruction." He wishes to establish labour exchanges and wants public employment—such as road-making—to be found for the unemployed.

He next conceives the idea of establishing communities similar to that of New Lanark. Then he proceeds to draw up a scheme for establishing home colonies of poor people. Land and capital is to be provided by the Government. This land is to be cultivated by the colonists, who are to maintain themselves and to use any surplus for paying off the capital invested and purchasing more land.

Parish and county authorities may be entrusted with the carrying out of his scheme.

He dwells on the importance of the land, and purposes to include workers as well as the unemployed in his scheme. Land is the only remedy for unemployment. Men must be able to supply their wants.

By September 1817 he is including all classes of

people in his scheme, and visualizing the whole world divided into self-supporting and self-governing communities. The communities in each country would owe obedience to some central government.

In 1819 he is soliciting capital for his scheme. His colonies are to have an agricultural basis, but they will be industrial as well.

He advocates a communal life, but he thinks it is possible for colonists to have their own goods and their own land.

A deputation from Leeds who visited New Lanark in 1818 pointed out that Owen recommended agricultural colonies, although his own establishment was a colony of manufacturers. His insistence on the importance of the land grew steadily stronger.

It is evident that Owen's economic thought was largely shaped for him. He was not an original thinker. His work at New Lanark was to some extent a development of Robert Dale's, his educational theories were those of contemporary thinkers. Much of his economic thought is a distorted reflection of that of Malthus and of Ricardo.

Place helped Owen to correct the MS. of his fourth essay, and James Mill is also supposed to have assisted.[1] Owen does not acknowledge this obligation, but he says that his scheme to relieve unemployment was originally one similar to that of John Bellers, published in 1696. Place gave Owen the tract in

[1] Podmore, i, p. 121, quotes from Graham Wallas, " Place," and Holyoake, " History of Co-operation," 1st edition, i, p. 57. Professor Graham Wallas, " Place," p. 63, quotes from Place : " He [Owen] introduced himself to me 1813 . . . he produced a MS. which he requested me to read and correct for him. I went through it carefully and it was afterwards printed."

1816. He thought that it would interest him, as it contained a scheme for " nationalizing the poor." [1]

Bellers' scheme was to purchase land in order to found colleges for poor people.[2] The poor people were to support themselves by means of their land and manufactures, and the profits were to go to the rich people who had invested their money in the undertaking. The scheme was not to relieve unemployment, nor was it for any particular time of distress.[3] It was simply a scheme to make it profitable for the rich to help the poor. Owen was bound, therefore, to modify this scheme.

He was inspired also by accounts of what the Rappites and Shakers had done in the New World. But these had founded religious societies in which marrying and giving in marriage were prohibited.[4]

Owen could not, therefore, cut his cloth strictly to the pattern of either Bellers or the Rappites and Shakers. What other patterns did he use ?

Podmore thinks, on the ground of similarity,[5] that he certainly owed some of his ideas to Spence. The similarity is sufficiently striking, as the brief summary of Owen's publications from 1812–20 shows. His

[1] J. Bellers, " Proposals . . . College of Industry," 1695. Republished 1696. Owen used this.
[2] Owen refers to this gift of a tract 120 years old, Autobiography Supplementary Appendix, Ia, No. 2, p. 77, and Ia, No. 3, p. 112.
[3] Podmore, i, p. 236.
[4] Reports of these communities had been appearing since 1812. E.g. John Mellish, " Account of a Society of Harmony . . . Pennsylvania taken from Travels . . . in 1806, 07, 09, 10, 11," from *Philanthropist*, xx. John Mellish, 1818, " Morris Birkbeck Letters from Illinois." George Courtauld, 1820, " Address to those who may be Disposed to Remove to U.S.A." 8vo. R. Owen, 1818, " Tracts Relative . . . Account of Shakers."
[5] Podmore, i, pp. 221–2.

idea of an England mapped out into small self-governing communities, bound together by a central government, closely resembles that of Spence. He even
suggests that they might be established by the county
or parish authorities. Owen recognizes the right of
the colonist to his personal property, to a share of
the profits, and to the capital contributed. Spence
would leave the members of the parish free to rent
land and acquire what wealth they could from their
farm or their trade. Both insist on military training.
Owen wants to " nationalize " the poor, Spence wants
the nation to assist in their maintenance. Both are
interested in education of a Godwinian type, and think
the communities should each be responsible for the
education of its members. Both want the local
authorities to have granaries and storehouses as a
provision against famine.

But it is their basic principles that really establish
a connection between the two men. Both believe
that the producer should have control of his produce,
that the sources of the country's wealth and the
control of that wealth should not be left in the hands
of a few private individuals. Both believe that this
end can be achieved by a system of local government,
the unit of which is the parish and its inhabitants,
or the community of five hundred to one thousand
souls with the land necessary for their support.

Owen is developing Spence's thought, for the latter,
in confining himself to small communities of farmers,
was solving only half the problem. How would
Spence's scheme apply to the industrial part of the
community ? Taking as his unit a community of

three hundred men, together with women and children, comparable to Spence's parish, Owen works out a solution that would include the town labourer. If the colony is to be self-supporting, there must be " manufacturers." The question at once arises, " Is not the industrial labourer being divorced from the soil, from his subsistence, the very evil the colony is to remedy ? " Owen replies, let the land be held in common, and that difficulty will disappear. Each member of the community will render service for service, and so each will have a fair share of the produce. Mutual obligations can be adjusted by payment according to a labour measure of value. Spence rightly regards the rents as public money, which is to be used for the public. Owen expects that there will be a surplus profit—after payment of expenses and shares—which will be divided out amongst the members of the community or devoted to some useful public purpose.

Both schemes would involve nationalization of the land, though both writers fail to make that clear. Both deal inadequately with commerce either from the inter-national, or from the inter-communal, aspect of the matter.

It is necessary to place this connection between Spence and Owen beyond doubt, as Owen has nowhere mentioned any obligation to him, nor does he state that he has read any of his tracts. Robert Owen was just the man to assimilate another's ideas whilst in process of despising them. His son says that he was no student, that he glanced over books without mastering them, and usually dismissed them with,

" the radical errors shared by all men make books of little value."

He acknowledges his debt to Bellers and the Shakers, but makes no mention of Godwin, Place, and others, to whom he was certainly indebted.

He would not recognize that his ideas had anything in common with those of Spence. Podmore says that unconsciously Owen depreciates the work done by Dale at New Lanark. Hone angrily remarks, " No one has quite such a good opinion of himself as Mr. Owen." [1]

Owen was a successful man, courted by the rich, Spence a miserable pauper who could not keep out of prison ; while Owen's followers were rich and influential, Spence's were a wretched set of fellows, whose mischievous ideas and activities were a menace to society.

After 1816, it would have been unwise for a would-be reformer to associate himself with the Spenceans. Owen's reticence can thus be easily accounted for.

The similarity and the logical connection between the ideas of the two men have been shown. A consideration of the following facts supports this conclusion.

Owen was under the influence of Place, who knew Spence well. In later years Place confessed himself a Spencean in regard to land reform.[2] Malthus, another friend of Owen, was acquainted with the Spencean Plan. It is impossible to believe that Spence's Plan

---

[1] Hone, *Reformists' Register*, 1817, col. 156.
[2] Place to Whytoch, October 28, 1839. Quoted by Professor Graham Wallas.

did not come under discussion when Robert Owen was disputing with the friends whose economic principles he felt were inferior to his own. Perhaps Place presented him with some of Spence's tracts as well as with one of Bellers ! [1]

But even if the possibility of this be discarded, it must be remembered that no one could be in London during the years 1812–20 without knowing something of the Spenceans. Spence's death in 1814 and the activities of his friends were reported in the leading London papers, all extensively patronized by Owen. Robert Dale Owen says that the perusal of the London dailies formed the bulk of his father's reading.[2]

In fact, Owen himself says that, in 1819, he was travelling from London to the North and had reached Newark. Two gentlemen in the coach began to discuss Owenism, but they knew so little of it that Owen joined in to enlighten them, and a three hours' discussion ensued, at the end of which one gentleman, the brother of Sir Charles Gray, the Governor of Jamaica, remarked, " I am sure you are Spence, or else Owen." Owen adds that Spence was " the advocate at that time of an equal division of land." [3]

Thus, on his own showing, Owen knew something of him.

The similarity of Spenceanism and Owenism struck Owen's contemporaries, for the " Black Dwarf," 1817,

[1] Malthus criticizes Owen's plan, vide " Principles of Population," 1817, p. 280 and note (a). Vide also his " Principles of Political Economy," 1820, pp. 427–34, 437 ; 1836, ii, pp. 377, 380. Spence and Owen are not actually named in the " Political Economy." Vide Owen's " Autobiography," pp. 103–4, 129, 130, etc.
[2] Podmore, i, p. 109.
[3] Owen, " Autobiography," p. 227.

asks why Spence was persecuted and Owen encouraged
by the Government. "The Spenceans have had the
honour of suggesting a new Plan . . . and while the
two Evanses are lying in the gloom of a dungeon for
being Spenceans, and although poor old Spence was
persecuted until the hour of his death for his Spencean
doctrines . . . Mr. Owen with his Spencean Plan
advertises it through the country." [1]

Hone says that Owen's scheme is the "Spencean
doubly dipped." [2] A reviewer in the *Gentleman's
Magazine* says that Owen's scheme would result in
Spenceanism and then anarchy. Luckily for himself,
Owen was a rich man who could buy up 30,000 newspapers to post to every parish in the kingdom, who
could spend £4,000 in three months for advertisements,
who could travel to propagate his views, who could
afford to make practical experiments. One would
expect Spenceanism to be forgotten and the Spenceans
to look to Owen for the means of realizing their ideals.

Did the various groups of thinkers who adopted
Owen as their leader and styled themselves Owenites,
and then, after 1827, Socialists, include Spenceans?
There is direct and indirect evidence to show that
they did.

Allen Davenport, writing in 1826, says that it was
the engrossment of the public in Owen's schemes that
led to the abandonment of Spence's Plan. He himself
was ready to support Owen, but he preferred Spence's
Plan and thought it more practicable.

[1] "Black Dwarf," 1817, p. 415.
[2] *Reformists' Register*, August 23 and 30, 1817. Vide also
Podmore, i, pp. 231-2 and p. 240.

The letters from correspondents in the *Economist* (1821–22), a weekly paper edited by George Mudie, an Owenite, throw more light on the subject. The paper was founded to further the cause of co-operation. It is interesting because it shows the direction in which the thought of various groups of thinkers who had come under the influence of Godwin, Paine, Hall, Spence, Owen, and the Ricardian School was tending.

" Philadelphus " writes asking to be assured that Owen's scheme is practicable. He wants the objections of Mr. Malthus removed, and points out that Malthus considers Owenism allied to Spenceanism.

" I need not offer any apology," he writes, " for having thus pointed to the wrecks of former grand projects which merely excite ridicule when the wreck consists of the shattered pinnace of a crazy projector, but causes a mingled feeling of scorn and pity when they display the fragments of the stately fabrics in which numbers have occasionally embarked in quest of El Dorado. . . ." March 13, 1821.[1]

This letter points to the fact that those who might have been interested in Spenceanism were abandoning it for Owenism, and the reason is obvious. Owen had social prestige. Spence had none.

Hone, it may be remarked, says that the " plan of the Evanses was innocency itself compared with Owen's."[2]

In Volume II of the *Economist*, there are[3] letters from a certain " H. O." Owen had been

[1] *Economist,* i, No. 8, pp. 126–7.
[2] Hone, *Reformists' Register,* col. 191.
[3] *Economist,* ii, 49, p. 366.

offered some land for his project by a Mr. Hamilton, and this correspondent is very anxious to know what security there would be for subscribers [he was told in effect—faith !]. He is afraid that it might prove a failure. He gives Owen credit for an entirely original plan, for he says that in all associations of which he has read or heard there was always been " . . . some strange comfort, some ruling passion, some ideal good, which served to distinguish and detach them from the mass of mankind, and which during their little day of triumphant singularity operated as a bond of union to hold them together. The visionary theories of Plato, More, Harrison, and Hume, and of Godwin and Spence are founded on the well-known habits and propensities of human nature. . . ."

Evidently some of the *Economist's* readers believed, like Davenport, that Spenceanism was more practicable than Owenism. The letters serve to indicate a drift from Spenceanism to Owenism.

If a connection between Spenceanism and modern Socialism is to be proved, it is enough to show that Owen was transmitting Spenceanism to his followers. Yet it is natural to wonder whether any other connections can be established between the thought of Spence and that of later writers.

Professor Foxwell, in his Introduction to Anton Menger's " Right to the Whole Produce of Labour," says that Hodgskins, Gray, Thompson and Bray,[1] starting from Ogilvie and Hale, worked out the main body of socialist doctrine in the first half of the nineteenth century, and that their principles developed

[1] All Owenites.

in opposition to those of Ricardo and his school. Can any logical connection be discovered between Spence and these writers ?

" Owenism " was a name covering many shades of thought. William Lovett, the Chartist, writing to Place in 1839, says that he helped to spread knowledge of Owen's schemes, but that he only accepted a part of his teaching for himself.[1] Can any current of thought be traced between 1821 and 1850 that is distinctly Spencean ?

Beer says that in 1838–39 in the Chartist Movement the name of Spence was held dear. Austin, lecturing at Cambridge in 1829, stated that the working-class was not favourable to a system of private property —why not ?[2]

Ernest Barker, in summarizing modern Socialist thought, points out that it is land rather than capital which has been the objective of English Socialism. He refers to T. H. Green and Herbert Spencer as objecting to the English system of landed property, and to J. S. Mill as developing the idea that rent was " unearned increment." He quotes Spence, Patrick Dove, Russell Wallace, and Henry George, the advocate of the single tax, as land nationalizers. Barker points also to a new tendency in modern thought, the tendency to think of the group and the group-mind rather than of the individual and the individual mind. He instances Guild Socialism, Home Rule, Trade Unionism, the Church as a Corporation (Dr. Figgis's conception).[3]

[1] Beer, " British Socialism," i, p. 184. Place, 27791.
[2] Beer, " British Socialism," p. 279.
[3] "Political Thought in England from Herbert Spencer," H.U.L., pp. 182, 214.

There is a temptation to cry at once " Hail Spence ! " but the mere fact that homage is paid to him as a land nationalizer by Hyndman, Morrison Davidson, and others, would not justify the greeting.

It must be shown that there are currents of thought directly ascribable to Spence in the later Owenite Movement. The connection between English and German Socialism in the middle part of the century must be established, and an attempt made to follow up clues in Manchester and Bath. The completion of the task seems merely to await the gathering up of material. But whether the task is completed or not, the record of his life and the pamphlets that he has left should be sufficient to secure to Thomas Spence a conspicuous niche in the Temple of Fame.

APPENDIXES

THE WRITINGS OF THOMAS SPENCE

A. *BIBLIOGRAPHY*
B. *COMMENTS ON THE BIBLIOGRAPHY*

A. BIBLIOGRAPHY [1]

A BIBLIOGRAPHY of Thomas Spence is necessary, because interest in Spence himself demands one and because an accurate list and description of his writings is important, not only to those who are concerned with Spence's own life and thought, but to those who are studying the history and development of modern socialistic thought. Unfortunately, several of the pamphlets, broadsides, and handbills, which constitute his writings, have disappeared, and several are undated. The bibliography, therefore, is imperfect.

[1] "The Bibliography "A" was published in the "Bulletin" of the London School of Economics in May 1926. The editor has kindly allowed me to insert it here.

NEWCASTLE PUBLICATIONS

1775.

"THE GRAND REPOSITORY"

of the English Language containing besides the excellencies of all other dictionaries and grammars of the English tongue, the peculiarity of having the most proper and agreable pronunciation of the alphabetic words denoted in the most intelligible manner by a new alphabet, with a copper-plate exhibiting the new alphabet both in writing and printing characters, intended for the use of everyone whether native or foreigner that would acquire a complete knowledge of the English language with the least waste of time and expense but especially for those who are but indifferent readers from not having been taught to pronounce properly.

By Thomas Spence, Teacher of English in Newcastle, Newcastle-upon-Tyne.

Printed by T. Saint for the Author and sold by him at his school in the Keyside, and by all the Booksellers in Town and Country. 1775."

380 pages.
Oblong. 12mo.

There is a copy of this in the Newcastle Public Library.

Pages unnumbered.

" Just published by the Author and sold by him at his School on the Keyside and by the Booksellers and News-Carriers,

No. 1. (Price one Penny) of

THE REPOSITORY OF COMMON SENSE AND INNOCENT AMUSEMENT.

In extracts from the best authors in which every word is spelled according to the best pronunciation by the new alphabet. Designed chiefly for those who cannot spare time, expense, and patience sufficient for learning to read and spell in the usual way. It will be continued weekly as soon as a competent number of subscribers is obtained. . . ."

Adertisement in grand Repository. Follows Preface.

1779. " THE POOR MAN'S ADVOCATE."

" Rights of Man as exhibited in a lecture read at the Philosophical Society in Newcastle."

Vide " Pigs' Meat," ii, p. 52. " Lessons for the Sheepish Multitude," which is stated to be from a pamphlet entitled the " Poor Man's Advocate," published at Newcastle by T. Spence, 1779.

1782. " THE REAL READING MADE EASY

or foreigners' and grown-up persons' pleasing introductor to reading English whereby all persons, of whatever age or nature, may soon be taught with ease and pleasure to read the English Language.

Illustrated Spence's system of phonetics. In Newcastle Public Library.

Printed and Sold by T. Saint. Newcastle. 1782.
Price one Shilling.
6 pages.
24mo.

Illustrates Spence's phonetics and Plan. In Newcastle Public Library.

"A S'UPL'IM'INT TOO THI HISTIRE OV ROBINSIN KRUZO.

Printed and Sold by T. Saint. Newcastle. 1782."
Price 6d.
Preface, iii, iv.
Pages 7–59.
24mo.

"A SUPPLEMENT TO THE HISTORY OF ROBINSON CRUSOE,

being the History of Crusonia or Robinson Crusoe's Island down to the present time, Copied from a letter sent by Mr. Thomas Wishit, Captain of the Good Intent to an intelligent friend in England, after being in a storm in May 1781, driven out of his course to the said island. Published by this said gentleman for the agreeable perusal of Robinson Crusoe's friends of all sizes.

An edition of the above in ordinary spelling. In Newcastle Public Library.

'The Invention all admired and each how he
To be the Inventor missed, so easy it seemed
Once found, which yet unfound most would have thought
Impossible.'

MILTON.

Printed and Sold by T. Saint. 1782."
Newcastle.
Price 6d.
Pp. 5–64.
24mo.

1783.   "RIGHTS OF MAN IN VERSE."

[Quarto Sheet ?]

Vide Broadsides for 1796;
Spence's "Songs"; "Pigs'
Meat," ii, p. 102.

LONDON PUBLICATIONS

1792.   ' THE CASE OF THOMAS SPENCE, BOOKSELLER,

the Corner of Chancery Lane, London who was committed to
Clerkenwell Prison on Monday the 10th of December 1792 for
Selling the Second part of Paine's "Rights of Man," and a
bill of indictment found against him to which is added an
extract of a letter from His Grace the Duke of Richmond to

British Museum. Goldsmiths'
Library.

the Chairman of the Committee of the County of Sussex convened at Lewes, Jan. 18th 1783 for the purpose of presenting a petition to the House of Commons to take into consideration the unequal date of representation in Parliament, etc.

[Price three-pence.]

1792.

Pp. 3–16.

12mo.

1793. " THE CASE OF THOMAS SPENCE . . .

to which is added the affecting case of James Maccuddy a native of Ireland who was committed to Clerkenwell Bridewell for distributing certain seditious papers, where he died in a few days.

[Price three-pence.]

1793."

Pp. 3–16.

12mo.

John Ryland's Library, Manchester.

"BURKE'S ADDRESS TO THE SWINISH MULTITUDE."

12mo.

1793 ? Spence ? In verse. The verses were *printed for* T. Spence of No. 8, Little Turnstile, High Holborn. Advertised in " Pigs' Meat," vol. iii. British Museum.

1793.

"THE RIGHTS OF MAN"

as exhibited in a lecture read at the Philosophical Society in Newcastle to which is now added an interesting conversation between a gentleman and the author on the subject of the Scheme with the queries sent by the Rev. Mr. J. Murray to the Society in defence of the same. And a Song of Triumph for the People on the Recovery of their Long Lost Rights. The fourth edition. By T. Spence. Printed for the author and sold at the Corner of Chancery Lane, Holborn, 1793."

    Preface.
    Lecture, pp. 2–18.
    Conversation, pp. 19–35.
    Queries, pp. 36–38.
    Song, pp. 38–9.
    Quotation from Swift, p. 40.
    12mo.

British Museum. I.e. the "Jubilee Hymn."

"ONE PENNYWORTH OF PIGS' MEAT."

"To be continued weekly. One Pennyworth of Pigs' Meat or Lessons for the Swinish Multitude collected by the Poor Man's Advocate in the course of his reading for more than 20 years, intended to promote among the labouring part of mankind proper ideas of their situation and importance and of their rights and to convince them that their forlorn condition

British Museum, Goldsmiths' Library.

has not been entirely overlooked and forgotten nor their just cause unpleaded neither by their Maker nor by the best and most enlightened of men in all ages."

Vol. i.
Printed for T. Spence.
Pp. 284.
12mo.

"RIGHTS OF MAN BY QUESTION AND ANSWER." "Pigs' Meat," i, p. 98.

Poems {"Jubilee Hymn." "Pigs' Meat," i, p. 61.
{"A Song to be Sung a Hundred Years Hence." "Pigs' Meat," i, p. 42.

1794. "ONE PENNYWORTH OF PIGS' MEAT."

Vol. ii.
Pp. 284.
12mo.

"THE MARINE REPUBLIC." "Pigs' Meat," ii, p. 68.

"A FURTHER ACCOUNT OF SPENSONIA." "Pigs' Meat," ii, p. 205.

POEM: "RIGHTS OF MAN IN VERSE." 'Pigs' Meat," ii, p. 102.

1794. "LESSONS FOR THE SHEEPISH MULTITUDE."

"Pigs' Meat," ii, p. 32. British Museum. Goldsmiths' Library.

1795. "END OF OPPRESSION"

on a quartern loaf for twopence being a dialogue between an old mechanic and a young one concerning the establishment of the 'Rights of Man,' London. Printed for the author and sold by T. Spence, patriotic bookseller.

Price one penny.
Pp. 2-7.
12mo.

? 1795.
MS. notes of pamphlet's owner in the British Museum copy.
British Museum.

"END OF OPPRESSION"

being a dialogue between an old mechanic and a young one ... Man."

2nd edition.
Price one penny.
Pp. 3-12.
12mo.

? 1795.
"Quartern loaf for twopence" omitted, also "Jubilee Hymn." Three paragraphs extra.
British Museum. Goldsmiths' Library.

"RECANTATION OF THE END OF OPPRESSION."

Price one penny.
8vo.

British Museum.

A LETTER FROM RALPH HODGE TO HIS COUSIN THOMAS BULL," etc.

Pp. 1–12.
Letter, 1–6.

British Museum. Goldsmiths' Library.

" ONE PENNYWORTH OF PIGS' MEAT."

Vol. iii.
Pp. 284.
12mo.

Advertisement in " End of Oppression," 1st edition, three volumes of " Pigs' Meat" for sale, half-bound, 7s. 6d.

THE LECTURE.

" Pigs' Meat," iii, pp. 220–41.

POEMS { ON THE LATE BARREN PATRIOTIC MEETINGS.

" Pigs' Meat," iii, p. 57.

TWO NEWGATE SONGS.

" Pigs' Meat," iii, p. 249.

VERSE IN CAVE.

" Pigs' Meat," iii, p. 250. British Museum. Goldsmiths' Library.

" ONE PENNYWORTH OF PIGS' MEAT."

Vols. i–iii.
2nd edition.
12mo.

Advertisement in " End ..." 2nd edition, three volumes of " Pigs' Meat" for sale, boards, 2s. each volume. British Museum. Goldsmiths' Library.

1795. "THE COIN COLLECTOR'S COMPANION
being a descriptive alphabetical list of the modern provincial and other copper coins, No. 8, Little Turnstile, High Holborn, 1795."
Pp. 1–50.
Supplement, pp. i–vi.
12mo.

British Museum. Goldsmiths' Library.

1796. "MERIDIAN SUN OF LIBERTY
on the whole rights of man displayed and most accurately defined in a lecture read at the Philosophical Society in Newcastle on 8th November, 1775, for the printing of which the Society did the author the honour to expel him, to which is now first added by way of preface, a most important dialogue between the citizen-reader and the author, by T. Spence."
Price one penny.
Pp. 2–12.
12mo.

British Museum. Goldsmiths' Library.

"REIGN OF FELICITY
being a plan for civilizing the Indians of North America without infringing on their national or individual independence, in a coffee house dialogue between a courtier, an esquire, a clergyman and a farmer."
Printed for T. Spence.
Price one penny.
Pp. 1–12.
12mo.

Goldsmiths' Library.

"A FRAGMENT OF ANCIENT PROPHECY

relating as some think to the present Revolutions [being the fourth part of the 'End of Oppression'] and 2 odes by P. Pindar." 1796.

Price one penny.
Pp. 3–12.

British Museum.

"PIGS' MEAT."

Vols. i–iii.
3rd edition.
12mo.

Goldsmiths' Library.

797. "RIGHTS OF INFANTS

or the imprescriptible Rights of Mothers to such a share in the elements as is sufficient to enable them to suckle and bring up their young, in a dialogue between the aristocrat and a mother of children, to which are added by way of preface and appendix strictures on Paine's Agrarian Justice, by T. Spence, No. 9, Oxford Street, lately removed from No. 8, Little Turnstile, High Holborn." 1797.

Price two pence.
Pp. 3–16.
8vo.

British Museum.

1793-97.   BROADSIDES AND SLIPS.

"Rights of Man " in verse and other poems.
                    Prices 1d. and ½d.

1798. " CONSTITUTION OF A PERFECT COMMONWEALTH."

" The Constitution of a Perfect Commonwealth amended and
rendered entirely conformable to the whole rights of man. Finis
coronat opus the second edition with a preface how to study
politics by T. Spence, author and publisher of that best repository of sound and standard politics entitled ' Pigs' Meat,'
and of several tracts on the imprescriptible rights of Mankind."
                    Price three pence.
                    18 pages.
                    12mo.

British Museum. Goldsmiths'
Library.

1801. " RESTORER OF SOCIETY TO ITS NATURAL STATE."

" A series of letters to a fellow citizen," " with a preface containing the objections of a gentleman who perused the MS.
and the answer by the author."   1801.
                    Price one shilling.
                    41 pages.
                    8vo.

Place, Add. MSS., 27808.

1803.   " RESTORER . . . STATE."

                    Pp. 3-84.

Printed in Spence's Phonetics.
Pamphlet as used for his
defence.

"CONSTITUTION OF SPENSONIA."
"A country in Fairyland, situated between Utopia and Oceana." Constitution "brought thence by Captain Swallow."
4th edition.
Pp. 1-27.

Printed in Phonetics. Published in the "Trial," together with the "Restorer."

"THE IMP'ORTANT TRI'AL OF TOMIS SP'ENS," together with the indictment.

Pp. 3-84.
Indictment, pp. iii-x.
12mo.

A second edition of the trial in ordinary spelling may also have been published this year. Indictment is in ordinary spelling. British Museum. Goldsmiths' Library, Guildhall.

1803. BROADSIDES: "SOMETHING TO THE PURPOSE."
2nd edition.
Price one penny.
s. sh. fol.

British Museum gives 1805 for this. Goldsmiths' Library.

1803. COLLECTION OF SONGS.

? 1803. Goldsmiths' Library.

1805. BROADSIDE: "WORLD TURNED UPSIDE DOWN."

1807. COLLECTION OF SONGS.
8vo.

? 1807. Goldsmiths' Library.

1807. "THE IMPORTANT TRIAL OF THOMAS SPENCE
for a political pamphlet entitled the Restorer of Society to its
Natural State, on May 27th, 1801, at Westminster Hall, before
Lord Kenyon and a special jury."

    2nd edition.

        Pp. 1–94.

        "Restorer" and defence, pp. 8–68.

        "Constitution of Spensonia," pp. 70–92.

        Indictment, pp. 3–7.

        8vo.

In ordinary spelling. Gold-smiths' Library.

"THE IMPORTANT TRIAL . . . ."

    12mo.

This is also a second edition. Goldsmiths' Library. British Museum.

1814. "THE GIANT-KILLER

or Anti-Landlord, No. 1, Sat. Aug. 6th, 1814. Price 4d.
This weekly miscellany besides supporting its title as to politics
will comprise humorous and instructive essays, remarkable
adventures, general anecdotes, moral tales, Historical and
Biographical sketches, poetry, etc., both original and from the
works of the best authors, frequently accompanied with appropriate remarks and observations, being on the whole a general
repository of elegant useful and amusing literature."

        Pp. 1–8.

        No. 2, Saturday, August 13th, pp. 9–16.

        No. 3, Saturday, August 20th.

Place, Add. MSS., 27808.

PERSONAL

1780. Verse in Miners' Cave.

1782. Advertisement in *Newcastle Courant*, January 12th. "Pigs' Meat," iii, p. 250.

1787. Advertisement in *Newcastle Courant*, December 7th. ?

1794. Letter in *Morning Post*, December 18th.

1795. Letter in *Chronicle*, January 3rd.

1796. "Democrat" to Spence, May 17th. Letter on reverse of title-page of "Fragment . . ."

1801. Copy in MS. of letter from Spence to Mr. Panther, Salop Gaol, November 20th.

1807. Correspondence with Charles Hall:
  1. Hall to Spence, June 12th, "3rd letter."
  2. Spence to Hall, June 28th, "6th letter."
  3. Spence to Hall, August 13th, "7th letter."
  4. Hall to Spence, August 25th, "8th letter."

    All in Place Collection. Add. MSS., 27808.

1808. Constable to Spence—letter—July 27th. MS. "Of Nobility."

UNTRACED WRITINGS

1775–92. The 1st,* 2nd and 3rd editions of the lecture.

1795. " REPOSITORY OF COMMON SENSE . . ." *

? " PRONOUNCING AND FOREIGNERS' BIBLE containing the Old and New Testament being, not only the properest book for establishing a uniform and permanent manner of speaking, the most sonorous, harmonious and agreeable English and also infinitely preferable to any introductory book hitherto contrived for teaching children or grown persons upon whose mother-tongue it is, *but* is likewise peculiarly calculated to render English universal, for by this book foreigners of any country may be taught to read English much easier than their own respective languages ; recommended as the most proper book for Sunday Schools, by T. Spence, Teacher of English, London." Printed by Cook and Debrett. 8vo.

Place, Add. MSS., 27808.

After 1783. " Spensonia."

1794. " EYE-SALVE " or political knowledge for the people entirely similar to " Pigs' Meat," and published likewise in penny numbers, will immediately commence, by T. Spence, at No. 8, Little Turnstile, Holborn.

Advertisement at the end of " Pigs' Meat," vol. ii.

1795-96.   "END OF OPPRESSION."   Part II.

1797.   DICTIONARY OF THE SPENSONIAN LANGUAGE.

1798.   "CONSTITUTION OF A PERFECT COMMONWEALTH."
        1st and 3rd editions.

N.B.—The third edition of a "Constitution of a Perfect Commonwealth," "revised and corrected, is reprinted in the same
size as these letters to which it will be a most suitable companion
and render the subject entirely complete."   Advertisement on
reverse of last page of "Restorer."   1801.

1803.   "CONSTITUTION OF SPENSONIA."
        1st, 2nd and 3rd editions.

1805.   BROADSIDE: "WORLD TURNED UPSIDE DOWN." *

1814.   "GIANT-KILLER," No. 3.*

* Inserted in the Bibliography, as there is some evidence of publication.

B. COMMENTS ON THE BIBLIOGRAPHY

It will be seen from the Bibliography that the British Museum Library and the Goldsmiths' Library possess the best collections of Spence's tracts. There are others in the Guildhall, the John Rylands Library, Manchester, and the Newcastle Public Library. Other public libraries may also have copies. No doubt private collectors also have specimens of them. Perhaps the missing tracts may yet come to light. The British Museum has the advantage of possessing the Place MSS. Place had collected material for a Memoir on Spence (Add. MSS., 27808), and thanks to this it has been possible to supplement and check the present list.

Before 1792, Spence's writings were published in Newcastle, and after that date in London. T. Saint was his publisher in Newcastle, Seale and Bates of 160, Tottenham Court Road, were, usually, his London publishers. His writings fall into two main groups, those which illustrated and advertised his new alphabet, and those which illustrated and advertised his new Constitution. To the former belong :—

" THE GRAND REPOSITORY."
" THE REPOSITORY OF COMMON SENSE AND INNOCENT AMUSEMENT."
" THE REAL READING MADE EASY."
" A S'UPL'IM'INT TOO THI HISTIRE OV ROBINSIN KRUZO."
" PRONOUNCING AND FOREIGNERS BIBLE."

"DICTIONARY OF THE SPENSONIAN LANGUAGE."
"DHE IMP'ORTANT TRI'AL OV TOMIS SP'ENS."

The subject-matter of the "S'UPL'IM'INT" and
"DHE IMP'ORTANT TRI'AL" should relegate these
two tracts to the second group, but as Spence published editions of them both in ordinary spelling, they
can be considered here with the others simply as
illustrating his system of phonetics.

"The Grand Repository" begins with a preface of
12 pages, explaining his reasons for inventing this
system of phonetics. "A Concise and Comprehensive
English Grammar" (9½ pages) follows, then the new
alphabet, e.g. "ᴧă ă as in Man (MᴧN)" (1 page),
the copperplate, a duplicate page of the alphabet, and
lastly the dictionary (348 pages). The words are
arranged in double columns, and there are 20 to 25
words a column.

E.g. A'bacus (ᴧBᴧKIS) n. a counting table, the
uppermost member of a pillar.

The advertisement of the "Repository of Common
Sense . . ." is immediately after the Preface in the
"Grand Repository."

According to the advertisement, it was a weekly
paper containing extracts from the writings of the
"best authors," and was evidently a predecessor of
Spence's better-known London publication "Pigs'
Meat." It must have had an existence, as Mackenzie
says that the "Repository of Common Sense . . ."
was published at his school and sold in penny numbers.
Many of his publications were sold in single numbers
and then bound into volumes. The "Real Reading
Made Easy" was sold separately, price one shilling,

but was afterwards bound with the " Supplement
. . . Crusoe." [1] This reading-book consists of extracts
from the Bible written in the " Crusonian " (later
" Spensonian ") manner.

> Ese Lesing fir Krusonein Skolirz.
> The'r Lord he iz the God.

At the end of the phonetic version of the " Supplement . . ." there is a proposition for printing the
whole Bible in the Crusonian manner when sufficient
subscriptions have been raised. Three octavo sheets
are to be published weekly, price 6d. Subscriptions
are invited from those who can only pay one penny
per week. The names of subscribers were to be
printed, and those who " concurred with the editor
in diffusing the glorious light of Revelation more
universally," and who helped him to " conserve the
project " which he had brought to such perfection,
were to have thirteen copies for the price of a dozen.

Place has a sample of this publication.[2] It is
undated, but probably belongs to Spence's first years
in London. The title-page states that it is by " T.
Spence, Teacher of English, London." It is printed
by Cook and Debrett. Probably he would not have
secured the services of these printers after he became
immersed in " politics." His misfortunes would make
him too poor to employ them. There is no record of
his having been a teacher in London, nor does he
refer again to himself as a teacher. It is likely, then,

[1] Vide Place, Add. MSS., p. 169. Place's description of the
little volume " Supplement . . . Crusoe," lent to him by Hone,
exactly fits the " Supplement . . . Crusoe " in the Newcastle
Public Library.
[2] Place, Add. MSS., 27808, p. 172.

that Spence published this soon after his arrival in London (1792), when he was still hoping to resume his old profession.

The title-page is properly set out, and on the back is a preface and an alphabet. Seven pages only are printed, the eighth is blank. The number contains the first seven and part of the eighth chapter of Genesis in phonetics. Each page is divided into two columns. The margins are covered with MS. notes in Spence's handwriting. This number, then, would seem to be a proof. Whether any numbers were actually published and sold either in Newcastle or in London is doubtful.

Hone told Place that about 1797 Spence was preparing a dictionary of the Spensonian language.[1] Most probably this would be a revision of the dictionary already published by him in Newcastle ("Grand Repository . . ."). No trace of this dictionary has been found.

The "Supplement . . . Crusoe" in the Newcastle Public Library, and that described by Place (the volume had been lent to him by Hone), is a small volume in 24mo, divided into three parts.

I. READING MADE EASY.

II. A S'UPL'IM'NT . . . KRUZO.

---

[1] Hone to Place, Add. MSS., 27808, p. 314.

III. A Supplement to the History of Robinson Crusoe, etc.

This volume is evidently a collection of Spence's chief publications. The parts of Nos. II and III may all have been sold as separate numbers. The price of the " History . . . Lilliput " was 6d.

Place thinks that II, the phonetic version, was published before III. This may be so, as Spence has put the phonetic version first, but it is a moot point.

The following advertisements appear in the *Newcastle Courant* (T. Saint) for Saturday, December 22, 1781, and Saturday, January 12, 1782.

This day is published, price 6d. bound, Printed and Sold by T. Saint. A Supplement to the History of Robinson Crusoe. Being the History of Crusonia or Robinson Crusoe's island down to the present time. Designed as an agreable New Year's gift for 1782 to all Ronson Crusoe's admirers.

Just published. Price 6d. bound . . . time. This book is printed and planned as to be the best adapted for a Reading-made-Easy . . . Mr. Spence, Teacher of English in St. Ann's School, Newcastle. Extracts on it. . . .

The second advertisement obviously refers to the phonetic edition. Either the two versions were published within three weeks of one another, in which case the phonetic edition came second, or the two advertisements both announce the publication of the phonetic edition. The edition in ordinary spelling must have followed later in 1782. One fact points to the first of the two alternatives—the " Supplement " in ordinary spelling has several charming little woodcuts to illustrate the various tracts. The frontispiece is a woodcut of Robinson Crusoe himself. The illustrations make it seem probable that this was the " New Year's gift."

Apparently Spence published little from 1783-92. In a list of Saint's publications for December 1784, " The wonderful life and surprising adventures of that renowned hero Robinson Crusoe who lived 28 years on an uninhabited island which he attverwards colonized " is advertised, price 6d. But there is nothing to show that this is not a cheap edition of Defoe's " Robinson Crusoe."

Except for an occasional broadside, Spence made little use of his phonetics in London. He printed an account of his " Important Trial," 1801, in phonetics to interest his friends. This edition appeared in 1803.

Spence's political writings may be conveniently dealt with in groups. There are the various editions of his lecture, his conversations and queries, his letters, his Utopias, his trials, his periodicals, his songs, broadsides and advertisements, his MSS.

There are three editions of the lecture extant, the fourth edition, 1793, the edition in " Pigs' Meat," vol. iii, p. 220, and " The Meridian Sun of Liberty," 1796. In his " Case of T. Spence," 1792, Spence says that he was selling his " Rights of Man " then, so that the second and third editions may belong to the year 1792. According to Place, he reprinted the lecture in that year, and from what Place says there can be little difference between the 1792 and 1793 versions.

There is no doubt that the first edition was published in 1775. Spence himself states this to have been the case. " The Meridian Sun of Liberty " is declared to be " the whole rights of man . . . defined in a lecture read at the Philosophical Society in Newcastle on 8th Nov., 1775." The Preface says: " Read this Lecture which I have been publishing in various editions for more than twenty years." In Letter XII of his pamphlet " Restorer of Society," written in 1800, he says that he has been publishing his lecture for five and twenty years, while at his trial in 1801 he told the Court that he first of all formed his opinions into a lecture which he read to the Philosophical Society and which he " immediately printed." Spence could not have made deliberate misstatements nor could he have forgotten an event which had such disastrous effects upon himself ; he could forget neither his expulsion from the Philosophical Society nor the occasion of it. It is as well, however, to have corroboratory evidence. Mackenzie, the Newcastle bookseller who wrote a special Memoir of Spence,[1] says that he published his new Constitution in 1775. Place thinks that Mackenzie is in error, as the latter attributes Spence's expulsion from the Society to his having hawked his lecture about the streets and printed it in the manner of a halfpenny ballad. He thinks that as the lecture is too long to be published in this form, Mackenzie must be con-

[1] Mackenzie, " Memoir of Spence," 1826.

fusing it with Spence's verse productions. But the objection can hardly stand, as Mackenzie must simply mean that the Society objected to the catch-penny form and method of propagation. Thomas Bewick, Spence's friend, and Mitchell, editor of the *Newcastle Magazine*,[1] both attribute his expulsion to his having printed and circulated the lecture which he had read. Sir M. W. Ridley stated in Parliament, 1817, that he had been a member of the Society to which Spence had read his paper, that Spence had published it a few days after, and that the paper was about thirty years old. Sir John E. Swinburne's secretary, writing February 23, 1817, gives Sir John's knowledge of Spence. Sir John said that the paper was about forty years old.[2] Amongst Place's papers is a MS. list of queries addressed by the Rev. J. Murray " to the Philosophical Society in Newcastle, December 26th, 1775." They were occasioned by Spence's expulsion. Spence published them in his " Rights of Man," 1793.

The 1793 edition of the lecture was entitled the " Real Rights of Man . . .," the 1796 edition the " Meridian Sun of Liberty." Mackenzie says that the 1775 edition was entitled the " Real Rights of Man." But Spence claims to have originated the phrase " Rights of Man " in the verse that he wrote on his visit to the Miners' Cave in 1780.[3] Place is doubtful whether his claim is good, as he only made it after Paine had published his " Rights of Man." Thousands of people must have used this phrase before Paine

[1] Bewick, " Memoirs." Mitchell, *Newcastle Magazine*, in Place, Add. MSS., 27808, pp. 315–18.
[2] " Southey's Essays," 1832, i, p. 97, note.
[3] Vide " Pigs' Meat," iii, p. 250.

appropriated it for a title. Spence duly claims it as a phrase used by him in a verse, not as the title of some publication, so probably the 1775 edition had a different title.

The 1793 edition includes the " Interesting Conversation," the " Queries " and the " Jubilee Hymn." The " Pigs' Meat " edition has the "Conversation" and the " Queries." A conversation between the Citizen-Reader and the Author prefaces the " Meridian Sun. . . ." The text of the three versions varies, that of 1796 having some important additions and omissions.[1]

The conversations and queries, included with these editions of the Lecture, are intended to throw additional light on the problem Spence is solving. This question and answer method of dealing with difficulties suggested to him by himself and his critics was then fashionable. The " Restorer of Society " has for preface a series of objections to his scheme in question form together with Spence's answers. There are " Queries " attached to an odd number of " Pigs' Meat," the " Letter to Ralph Hodge . . ." In " Pigs' Meat," vol. i, p. 261, there is a catechism, " The Rights of Man by Question and Answer." This catechism is anonymous, but the style and matter show that Spence must have been the author.[2]

The " Lesson for the Sheepish Multitude " in " Pigs' Meat," vol. ii, pp. 32–35, consists of " Queries of Importance."

---

[1] The chief variations in the text of the three editions are given in a separate table, pp. 250–251.
[2] The remarks " by a Spensonian " (" Pigs' Meat," i, p. 188), on an extract from Sir J. Sinclair's writings, are obviously Spence's.

E.g., In Spensonia, where land is public, would people with much money have more reason to complain than people with a little money because they could buy land ?

Or, Ought a man rich with trade to complain because he cannot deprive men of their land ?

These queries are from the pamphlet " The Poor Man's Advocate," published by Spence at Newcastle in 1779.   No trace of it has been found.

Several of his pamphlets are " conversations " on his new Constitution. His Plan is explained and discussed by their means.   " The Reign of Felicity," the " Rights of Infants," and the " End of Oppression " are pamphlets of this conversation type.   There are two editions of the " End of Oppression," both undated.   The words " or a quartern loaf for 2d." are omitted from the title-page of the second edition and a mistake in the dialogue is corrected.   The " young " mechanic is made to respond to his own remark on the felicity of landlords. This is set right.   Place says that the " End " was published in two parts, price 2d.   There is no trace of this second part, but the " Recantation of the End of Oppression " and the " Fragment of an Ancient Prophecy " are the third and fourth parts.

A first edition copy in the British Museum has some manuscript notes made by its former owner. He has written, " Pp. 6 and 7 cited by Lord Mornington in the House of Commons."   This note is on the front cover, and the parts to which he was drawing attention are marked.   He has noted, also, that the pamphlet is by Spence and that few copies of it were issued. He has added a short biographical note on the " poor deluded fellow." The second edition has three extra paragraphs.

The four parts of the " End of Oppression " must have been published during the years 1795 and 1796. There is no reference to them before 1794, and Spence was in prison from May to December 1794. The third volume of " Pigs' Meat " was completed in 1795, and the second edition of the " End of Oppression " has an advertisement which announces that the three volumes of " Pigs' Meat " are now bound ready for sale. The " End of Oppression " is itself advertised in the " Meridian Sun," 1796, and in the second edition of " Pigs' Meat," vol. iii, which may belong either to 1795 or 1796. It is most probable that the " End of Oppression " was published in 1795. If it were not, Spence must have been singularly quiet in 1795 and feverishly active in 1796. Possibly the " Recantation . . .," a mock renunciation of his schemes, belongs to the same year. The bitterness of tone in both pamphlets seems appropriate to that year, for he felt that he had been unjustly imprisoned in 1794, and that on his release he had been slighted by the very people he was trying to help. The advertisements of the " End of Oppression " in his 1796 publications were perhaps to stimulate a slow sale. He went bankrupt in 1797. The " Fragment . . . Prophecy," the fourth part of the " End of Oppression," is dated 1796. It prophecies in a scriptural form the establishment of his system. On the reverse of the title-page Spence has printed " The true copy of a letter that he has received."

Sometimes Spence made use of the letter as a literary form. An interesting example is his " Letter to Ralph Hodge. . . ." The edition of this letter in both the British Museum and the Goldsmiths' Library is bound with some duplicate numbers of " Pigs' Meat." As it is paged independently of these it must be an odd number. It does not appear in any of the three volumes of " Pigs' Meat." Besides the letter, there are some queries, and an extract from Volney's " Les Ruines " (in translation).

His pamphlet, the " Restorer of Society," consists of a series of letters which set forth his views. Place has preserved a copy of the first edition. It was this publication that resulted in Spence's " Important Trial." After his imprisonment, Spence republished the pamphlet as he had prepared it for his defence. Most of his comments and explanations are inserted as footnotes. The last of the letters was finished in December 1800, the first edition was published in 1801 ; the " Important Trial " was published 1803 and 1807.

Spence wrote various pamphlets to show how his Plan would work out in practice. His " Constitution of a Perfect Commonwealth," for instance, has as preface an article " How to Study Politics." He imagines his scheme being carried out in the parish of Little Dalby, Leicestershire.

The " Supplement to the History of Robinson Crusoe " is an account of the adoption of his Plan by the colony that Crusoe had established. He calls the island " Crusonia." In " Pigs' Meat," vol. ii, 1794, and in the " Giant-Killer " (1814), he published revised versions of this, divided in each case into two

parts, the first entitled " The Marine Republic," the
second, "A Further Account of Spensonia." The
three versions vary considerably from one another.
Place says that Spence published " Spensonia " after
the " Rights of Man in Verse " 1783. Possibly Spence
published an edition of " Spensonia " before he left
Newcastle.

" The Constitution of a Perfect Commonwealth "
is a translation of the French Constitution of June 24,
1793.[1] He has adapted this so as to form a constitution for Spensonia. On the back of the last page of
the " Restorer . . ." there is an announcement that
a third edition of the " Perfect Commonwealth " was
in preparation. The first edition very likely belongs
to the same year, 1798.

" The Constitution of Spensonia " is a development
of the " Perfect Commonwealth." There is a copy
included with each of the two editions of his " Important Trial." Both are " fourth " editions, though
one, like the rest of the pamphlet, is in the Spensonian
spelling. On the back of the title-page he explains
that Lord Kenyon had asked for a copy of the " Constitution," and so he had included it in his defence.
He also says that it appeared twice before the trial.
Place gives the date 1798–99. It must have succeeded
the " Perfect Commonwealth," and Spence was busy
with the " Restorer . . ." in 1800, so Place is probably
correct.

Spence was anxious that the public should know
of his persecutions, chiefly for the sake of the cause.

___

[1] " Acte Constitutionnel précédé de la déclaration des droits,
. . . Présenté au Peuple français le 24 juin 1793. . . ."

Accordingly, he published pamphlets in which he narrated his sufferings. The first of these is his " Case of T. Spence . . . 1792." Spence does not say that he is the writer of the pamphlet, but it reads as if it were a personal narrative, and the style is undoubtedly his. It was sold at the Corner of Chancery Lane where Spence had his stall. Place says that it is one of his publications.

A variant of this was published in 1793. The actual story is the same, but the reflections and rhetoric have been altered. The case of James Maccuddy has taken the place of the Duke of Richmond's letter. There is no mention of the Plan.

His *famous* trial was in 1801, and he published his defence in 1803. This edition is in the Spensonian spelling. A note in ordinary spelling at the end says : " This curious book is not printed for sale but only for a present of respect to the worthy people who contributed to the relief of Mr. Spence." He has omitted a copy of the indictment because of the expense, and he has also omitted the title-page of the " Restorer." A comparison of the number of pages in this edition with the number in the non-phonetic edition explains Spence's remarks on the cost. The phonetic edition included the " Restorer . . ." and the " Constitution of Spensonia." The indictment was published as a second part in ordinary spelling. He published another edition of the trial in 1807. The copies of this in the British Museum and Goldsmiths' Library have " second edition " on the title-page, but they are undated. There is another " second edition " in the Goldsmiths' Library, with

" Printed by A. Seale, Tottenham Court Road, 1807,"
on the back of the title-page. This edition is in 8vo.
The two other second editions are in 12mo, and may
have appeared in the same year as the first edition.
These second editions are in ordinary spelling. They
contain a copy of the indictment, the defence and
the " Restorer . . ." the " Constitution of Spensonia."
As in the case of the 1792 pamphlet, Spence is not
stated to be the author, but the use of phonetics in
the 1803 edition and the inclusion of the " Constitution
of Spensonia " show that he must be. His advertisements to the reader in the pamphlet and his later
references to it make " assurance doubly sure."

Spence propagated his doctrines by means of cheap
periodicals. His first ventures of this kind were
issued from his school. The " Repository of Common
Sense " was a weekly paper. It was issued to make
known his system of phonetics. The paper contained
" extracts from the best authors," and was evidently
the forerunner of the famous " Pigs' Meat," a penny
weekly, deriving its title from Burke's allusion to the
" swinish multitude." The numbers were afterwards
collected and sold bound into volumes. The notices
advertising the volumes explain that each consisted
of twenty-four penny numbers. There are 284 pages
in each, but the numbers are not marked off from one
another. There is an index at the end of each volume.
Apparently the editor, as Spence calls himself, was
the only contributor. There are a few anonymous
articles and a few poems and articles by Spence himself, otherwise the volumes consist of extracts from
well-known authors and poets—such nourishment as

the editor believed would be most suitable for the swinish multitude.

The papers in Volume I must have been in circulation during the latter part of the year 1793, those in Volume II 1793–94, and those in Volume III in 1795. The articles on pages 3 and 4 of Volume III help to fix the dates. Both are letters of Spence, one had been printed in the *Morning Post* for December 18, 1794. He tells the editor that the second volume of " Pigs' Meat " " was finished on that memorable day, the 17th of May, 1794." The other is a letter which appeared in the *Morning Chronicle*, January 1795. Spence asks his fellow-citizens to help him sell " Pigs' Meat."

From the advertisements in the volumes it is clear that there was no long interval between the issue of the papers in Volume I and the issue of those in Volume II. At the end of Part I, Volume I, and Part I, Volume II, there are notices that the remaining parts of the work will be issued as before in penny numbers weekly, and at the end of Part II, Volume I, there are notices that the second volume will be issued as the first. As Volume II, then, was finished on May 17, 1794, and as each volume contained twenty-four numbers, Volume I must belong to 1793. Further, in Volume I, p. 163, there are two advertisements extracted from the *Morning Chronicle* for November 1793, and there is another on page 193 for the same date. A translation of a new Constitution for France the one adopted August (June) 1793, is given, and there are extracts from Godwin's " Political Justice." On pages 238–9 there is an extract dated December 16, 1793. Now the first number of Volume II should have been published December 7, 1793 (or November 30th if no paper was published in Christmas week), so the two issues must have overlapped.

Part I in each volume ends on page 144 (twelve numbers of 12 pages each), but there are only 140 pages in Part II. This points to irregularities in the times of publication of the papers and in the amounts of nourishment that they contained.

Volume III could not have appeared before 1795, as Spence was in prison from May to December 1794. The appeal for help in the selling of " Pigs' Meat " would refer to Volume II. The advertisements in the " Meridian Sun " and the " Fragment " (both 1796) announce that " Pigs' Meat " was finished and ready for sale in " three volumes duodecimo, price 2/6d. each, half-bound."

There are extracts in the volume dated 1795, but none 1796. Thus it is probable that Volume III belongs to the year 1795.

The title-page of Volume I has some quotations from the Psalms. In Volume II different quotations from the Psalms are given and the extracts are stated to have been collected by " . . . an old persecuted veteran in the cause of freedom." The title-page of Volume III is similar to that of Volume II, but the quotations from the Psalms are replaced by the following verse :—

> The Pigs to starve bad men in pow'r
> Their feeder sent to doleful gaol,
> But now the storm is blown o'er
> He feeds them with his wonted joy.

There is a " second edition " of " Pigs' Meat " in the British Museum. The three issues are bound in one volume. Volume I has " second edition " on the title-page. Page 67, which follows page 64 in the first edition, is in its right place, and the " Fable of the Bee and the Spider," missing in the first edition, is inserted. Volumes I and II have a woodcut of a pig as frontispiece with the legend :

> This is that matchless Pigs' Meat
> So famous far and near,
> Oppression's heart it fills with dread
> But Poor Man's hearts does cheer.

Volume III has a woodcut of Masaniello, the Neapolitan fisherman, coloured red and blue. Underneath are a few lines of verse in a reproduction of Spence's handwriting.

In the Goldsmiths' Library there are three sets of the three-volume edition of " Pigs' Meat." The first volume of one set is marked " second edition," and the first volume of each of the other two sets " third edition." As all the volumes bear his Holborn address, they must have been published before 1797, so that the second and third editions belong to the years 1795 and 1796. The " second edition " in the Goldsmiths' Library is similar to that in the British Museum, except that it is in three volumes. (Spence says in his advertisements that the numbers were bound both ways.) " Masaniello " faces page 22 in the third edition. In one set of the third edition Volume II has lost its frontispiece, the pig, and Volume III has some additional poems at the end. In each of

Volumes I and II of the other third edition set one of
Spence's broadsheets has been inserted.

The odd pages of "Pigs' Meat," to which reference
has already been made, are pages 97, 102, and 108 of
Volume II. They are evidently odd pages escaped
from or not bound in their proper volume. The odd
number, the "Letter to Ralph Hodge . . ." has 12
pages, the letter occupying the first 6. At the end
there is an announcement that "Pigs' Meat" is
complete in two volumes, price sewn 4s., consisting of
48 numbers at 1d. singly. Bound volumes could
be purchased, or the numbers could be obtained
singly. The date of this letter must be 1795, as no
reference is made to Volume III. It is directed against
informers, and therefore probably has some connection
with his imprisonment in 1794.

At the end of "Pigs' Meat," Part I, Volume II,
Spence advertises that he is about to publish a new
penny weekly, "Eye-Salve." He must have abandoned this project, as there is no other trace of it.
His next weekly publication was the "Giant-Killer
or Anti-Landlord." Thomas Evans, Spence's friend
and biographer, says that three numbers of this
appeared. Spence's death put an end to the publication. Place has preserved Nos. 1 and 2, that for
Saturday, August 6th, and Saturday, August 13th.

No. 1 sets forth by way of introduction the
aim of the paper : "To enquire into the possibility
of doing without so expensive and burdensome a
class (i.e. of landlords) is the main design of this
paper." Then follows the first part of "Spensonia,"
"The Marine Republic," a revised version of the

account in " Pigs' Meat," "An Infallible Way to Cure Provinciality and other Vulgarisms in Speech "; remarks on the prophetic records (Revelation), a letter on the slave trade, " The Old Man's Guide to Health," " Innocence and Guilt," a quotation from Fielding, " From Desmond a Novel " (evils of feudal system), civilization of the Cherokee Indians, " Terrors by Night " (a humorous anecdote), a page of poems. No. 2 has a letter, " Of the art military and the origin of nobility," letter on landlords, the continuation of "Spensonia," a warning to lawyers, a Chinese society of levellers, an interesting fact from the history of the Island of Elba, a humorous anecdote, a page of poems.

The verses written by Spence were included in his various publications. Some were issued as broadsides. They generally have reference to his scheme, either by way of laudation or explanation. They are written to fit in with the music of well-known songs and ballads—" God Save the King," " Chevy Chase," " Rule Britannia," " Babes in the Wood." Besides being sold singly, the songs of Spence and of his disciples were collected and sold in one volume. There are two of these song-books in the Goldsmiths' Library. Both are undated. Each consists of three parts. Part I cost 2d., Parts II and III each cost 1d. Part I has 12 pages, numbered, and Part II 4 pages, unnumbered. Part III in one copy has 6 pages, in the other 9. The " Humourous Catalogue of Spence's Poems," which precedes Part I in the 6-page copy, is bound with Part III in the 9-page copy. The 6-page copy has a leaflet, " Spence's Plan," while the other

has " A New and Infallible Way to Make Peace,"
the " Marseilles Hymn " and the " Jubilee Hymn." [1]

These song-books were published after Spence's
imprisonment, 1801–02, as a poem written by Spence
in Salop Gaol is included (see Part II).   On page 3 of
Part I there is a reference to Spence's " Trial and
Constitution which may be had at the small price of
1s."   The song-book must have been published, then,
in 1803 or 1807.   The inclusion of the " Jubilee Hymn,"
the translation of the " Marseillaise," and the " New
and Infallible Way to Make Peace " in one copy suggests
that it was published 1802 or 1803.

As Spence issued tokens to advertise his Plan, it is
appropriate to mention here the catalogue of tokens
which he published in 1795.   This catalogue gives a
list of the various tokens in circulation, and includes
Spence's own.   There is a copy of it in the British
Museum with MS. additions to the list and notes.
One of the two copies in the Goldsmiths' Library has
MS. notes.   Many of the tokens are in the British
Museum, and there are reproductions of them in
Dalton and Hamer's " Provincial and Token Coinage
of the Eighteenth Century."

[1] The songs vary a little.   The " Jubilee Hymn " published with
the 1793 edition of the Essay has a different second verse from
that in " Pigs' Meat," i, p. 42.

1793.
The Parish Rate is all
Paid now by great or small
For house or land.

" PIGS' MEAT."
Welcome that day draws near
For then our rents we share . . .

Sometimes verse 31 of " Rights of Man in Verse " is omitted.
The " Touchstone of Honesty " in the 9-page copy of the " Songs,"
has one more verse than in the 6-page copy.

His broadsides contained selections from his songs or extracts from his pamphlets. " Burke's Address to the Swinish Multitude " was printed for T. Spence of No. 8, Little Turnstile, Holborn. It appeared during the years 1793–97, though probably it belongs to 1793, as it is a skit on Burke and contains a reference to Paine. Most likely these verses are not Spence's own—they seem too good. About this time he began to circulate his " Rights of Man in Verse." There is a political slip containing the song in the British Museum. Thirty out of the thirty-one 4-line verses are given. It is expressly stated that the verses were first published in 1783. The address given is No. 8, Little Turnstile, Holborn. The two broadsides inserted into Volumes I and II of " Pigs' Meat," third edition, are both " Rights of Man in Verse." That in Volume I has lost the last lines of the last verse and the notes explanatory of a reference to the Plan, as the sheet has been clipped in the wrong place. The one in Volume II has lost its title in the binding process but the bottom of the sheet is intact. The verses are the same as those in the British Museum slip and as in " Pigs' Meat," vol. ii, p. 102. One bears the date February 2, 1796, and the other February 1, 1796. Both state that the verses were first printed in 1783, both give the Little Turnstile address. In each case, however, the folio is headed " first published . . . by T. Spence now at No. 9, Oxford Street." They must therefore have been issued after his removal to Oxford Street early in 1797.

Each of these broadsides is adorned with a large coloured woodcut, and each is signed " W. Spence."

One is called the "Disappointed Missionary." A fat missionary is addressing some Red Indians (noble savages !).

"God has enjoined you to be Christians. Pay Rent and tithes and become a Civilized People."

RED INDIANS.

If Rents we once consent to pay
Taxes on us you will lay
And then our freedom's passed away.

The other broadside is entitled "The Contrast," and has a picture, this time of two Red Indians (left) and the Civilized Ass (right). The ass has two pairs of panniers. Attached to the ass is the legend :—

Behold the Civilised Ass
Two pairs of panniers on his back,
The first with Rents a heavy mass,
With taxes next his bones do crack.

Underneath the pictures are thirty verses of the "Rights of Man in Verse" in two columns. The Plan is briefly explained in the footnotes.

There are two political slips which belong to this period in the British Museum, "The Marseilles March or Hymn," a translation of the "Marseillaise" appropriated for his purpose, published at No. 8, and the "New Irish Song by Captain Morris" (Tune : "O dear, what can the matter be ? "). These verses express hostility to the war, and were "printed for T. Spence at the Hive of Liberty, No. 8, Little Turnstile, London, where a petition against the war lies to be signed."

After his release from gaol in 1802 Spence began to

issue broadsides again. One of these is entitled
"Something to the Purpose." The folio copy in the
Goldsmiths' Library and the one in the British
Museum have each a picture of two females, Justice
and Peace. Beneath this picture are articles from
the "Constitution of Spensonia." The price is one
penny. There is a "second edition" in the British
Museum. This has no picture, but it has an extra
article from the Constitution and some verses. His
address is given as Prince's Street, Soho, so that
they cannot be earlier than 1803. They are partly
in phonetics. His "world turned upside down," a
map of the world with the poles reversed, was dedicated
to Earl Stanhope. Place includes it in his list of
publications, and dates it November 30, 1805, the date
ascribed to it by Mackenzie. But there seems to be
no trace of it.

The handbills were generally notices of meetings or
advertisements of the Plan. The Report of the Secret
Committees and of Hansard, the magazines and newspaper articles describe their contents. "Spence's
Plan," a bill inserted in the 6-page copy of his "Songs,"
belong to the year 1816, is typical of these handbills. The "New and Infallible Way to Make Trade"
and the "New and Infallible Way to Make Peace,"
two of Spence's miscellanies included with the songs
in the song-books, are evidently handbills.

Some of Spence's MSS. survive. Place has an
essay in his handwriting "Of Nobility." The ink is
very brown, and the writing is that of an elderly man
whose penmanship has been acquired with difficulty.
Part of this essay is printed in the "Giant-Killer"

for August 13, 1814. The specimen of the Bible in the Place Collection has a copy of a letter written by Spence on the blank side of the last page. This is the letter to Mr. Panther. It is dated November 20, 1801, and was written in Salop Goal. Then there are Spence's letters to Hall and Hall's to Spence, all in the Place Collection. On the back of a letter to Place from R. C. Fair is written in pencil, " I have Spence's letter to Mill, do you want it ? A.B." But Place has not included the letter in his collection.

Spence says in his letter to the *Morning Post*, December 18, 1794, that " many thousands have read and as many thousands have approved this incomparable political instruction." [" Pigs' Meat."] In Letter XII of the " Restorer " he says that he has been diligently publishing his Plan for five and twenty years, and has sold many thousands of copies. He must, therefore, have sold a great many copies of each, but whether he really sold " thousands " cannot be proved. In the Home Office Papers there is a letter [1] dated May 17, 1797. The writer complains to the police that Spence's halfpenny ballads are being sold in the Marylebone Road. The police made an investigation. According to the deposition of the small boy employed by Spence, he was allowed 1s. 3d. of the takings. On an average he made 4s. per day. It is not clear whether this 4s. represents his net gains. If they are the gross takings, he must have sold ninety-six copies a day. He had been employed in this manner for two months. Another boy was similarly employed, presumably on the same terms.

[1] H.O., 119. 1.

If one of them sold at this rate for six days per week, the number of copies sold would run into thousands.

These are the only figures procurable. If the small boy was not exaggerating, then Spence's assertion that he sold thousands of some publications is warranted.

VARIATIONS IN THE TEXT OF THE THREE LECTURES.

Beer's Reprint.[1] Page	"Real Rights of Man." 1793.	"Pigs' Meat," III. 1795.	"Meridian Sun." 1796.
6	(1) Sustain himself and connexions.	Sustain himself and family.	As 1795.
	(2) Most selfish and corrupted.	As 1793.	Most selfish and corrupt.
8	They, like the creatures, were claimed.	They like the brutes were claimed.	As 1795.
9	By laws of their own making every living creature.	As 1793.	By laws of their own making, for they are the landlords alone who make the laws, oblige every living creature.
11	In paying the government its share of the sum which the Parliament or National Congress at any time grants.	As 1793.	In paying the government so much per pound to make up the sum which the Parliament or National representation at any time thinks requisite.
	"O Hearken . . . undertook"	not in these editions.	". . . own territories O Hearken ye besotted . . . undertook there instead of them . . ."

12	A certain number of neighbouring parishes as those in a town or county have each an equal vote in the election of persons to represent them in Parliament, Senate or Congress.	A . . . county choose delegates to represent them in Parliament, Senate or Congress.	A certain number of neighbouring parishes chose delegates to represent them in Parliament, Senate, or Congress.
13–14	. . . is discounted by the Exchequer.	As 1793.	. . . is deducted by the Parish out of the first payment made to the state.
14	Are looked upon with an envious eye.	As 1796.	Looked upon by their new neighbours where they have come to reside with an envious eye.
15	As all have property alike to defend.	As 1793.	As all have a property to defend.
15–16	Which . . . occupies in it. And the rents are still . . . government much expense.	As 1793.	Omitted.
	* . . . * not in	these editions.	Without tax or price *When houses, lands or any tenements . . . set them up again. Though I have only spoken . . . deprived of.* But what maker . . .

1 Beer, " Pioneers of Land Reform." Bohn's Classics.

INDEX